OUT OF THE COMFORT ZONE INTO THE SADDLE

A horseback journey through
South Western France

RUTH LEVY-SO

Cover design by Pablo Simo
ISBN - Paperback: 9798362575793
First Edition: December 2022

CONTENTS   Page number

CHAPTER 1

THE LIMOUSIN

So there I finally was at Portsmouth, England, in my Vauxhall Astra waiting in line to board the ferry to France. It was the 26th of April 2018 and a gorgeous, sunny spring day. Crystal clear blue skies shone above me on the deck as I watched the UK fade into the distance as we gracefully slid across the English Channel.

The trip was a combination of years of planning and yet failing to plan, at least till recently. For years, almost since I got him in 2005, I'd been dreaming of taking my beautiful Argentine Criollo horse Salvador for a long trail ride in another country.

We had thoroughly explored Dartmoor where I lived, riding through the beautiful, but rugged and sometimes bleak terrain and I longed to touch and taste a different, lesser known landscape on the back of my trusty steed. The beauty of travelling on horseback is that you get to see every square inch of God's land. You go at a pace where you are in harmony with the rhythm of nature and the great outdoors.

In a car you miss almost everything but on a horse you miss nothing and life is slowed down and makes sense again . It's a choice to live at this speed or to live at breakneck speed which is literally called that because if you continue it breaks you.

Riding on Dartmoor was always a summer pursuit for me. It's so wet and cold and muddy and even in summer the bogs can claim a horse. You have to learn to read the terrain, the plants and the feel of the moor. A bog can lurk beneath the dry, crusty surface of the ground.

I lived adjacent to the Two Moors Way, the route that links Dartmoor to Exmoor. I have heard it said that the difference between the two is that on Exmoor you can ride anywhere except where you can't ride but on Dartmoor you can't ride anywhere except where you can ride. I had to think about that for a while when I first heard it but it just about sums it up!

I chose to live there because I wanted to be free of enclosures and boundaries and in the UK, apart from Scotland and Wales there are not too many areas where you can ride for miles. I have always been passionately in love with horses. I don't know where it came from? My parents are not animal people. None of my living relatives were that I know of.

As a child, learning to ride was the highlight of my week. Going to the riding school and waiting to see "the list," of who you were mounted upon for your ride was heart stopping . Please let it be Black Prince or Paul, I silently implored. Not Big or Little Kitty, they were too quiet and too old. Then you would go for your hour's ride. I remember the huge grass verges with canter tracks up in East Yorkshire. There was so much empty space to ride in back then and I don't remember there ever being much traffic.

If on your return to the yard you were allowed to help "the girls" muck out or groom, you were the luckiest person alive. Eating my sandwiches in the hay barn was the best lunch. Really my Sundays back then were nothing short of ecstasy. As were all my horsey endeavours. I would seek any opportunity to involve myself with horses, any horses; old stallions belonging to old farmers, one time racehorses now in their retired dotage (I feel horses lived longer back then but that's another topic), friends who were lucky enough to have horses in meadows that sheltered under ancient oak trees and that are now the site of ugly ageing 1960's housing estates. I was even happy to take the odd outgrown or unrideable Shetland pony in my garden.

I felt sorry for my sister who was not really horsey and blighted by childhood asthma. Hay and straw would make her sneeze but I would have been happy to eat it if my mother had fed me it.

I was so mad about the creatures that my gang of likewise minded horsey friends and I played at being horses in breaktime at my all girls school. We were not only the horse but the rider too as we made a circle and trotted and cantered across the diagonal, changing the rein and legs freely. Just occasionally, if I am on my own on an erstwhile canter track, I might still do it but these days I keep my jumps tiddly.

I lived in a time when being Jewish in a church school made one so obviously different and it was not even disguised. But neither Judaism or Christianity offered me the sanctuary I found at the church of the horse and aside for a few breaks from riding to do important things like bear children, for the most part that has been my devoted religion.

I have done all sorts of riding and horsey things in my time, cross country, show jumping-at a very amateur level, never cared for dressage, bounced around indoor arenas, trotted around blocks. I have run yards and driven horses about the country.

I've often felt I don't belong but maybe that's not true. Many women will recognise our caste up and down the motorways of this country as we sit at the wheel of our trucks and lorries, rosettes hanging above our heads, eating chocolate, hauling our beloved four leggeds all over the country being handed coffee by our friends and makeshift grooms navigating in the passenger seat and possibly a few dogs coming along for the ride. The only thing that keeps us from being an organised group or society are often our husbands and horses, who are endless work. But we are a tribe. Women who love horses, perhaps too much.

I got to my 40's after somehow getting a degree and having three children and decided on a new direction in Equestrianism. The cowgirl in me beckoned. I took up Western riding but what really appealed to me was riding across the range like a frontier woman in America in the 1900's. But I was brought up riding in arenas and going for short hacks and knew nothing of long riding apart from a stirring in my soul that arose after my children were born. I was given a book as a present by their Dad one Christmas called, 'Great Horse Treks of the World' and I can honestly say it was one of the most inspiring presents I ever had as I pored over the amazing places to ride on this beautiful Earth. I hatched a plan for long distance riding albeit from an armchair. For me it fuses the perfect combination of riding and travelling which are my two greatest passions.

I ultimately wanted to join that small, unique band of adventurers that have been admitted into the circle that is the Long Riders guild. All you had to do to be accepted was to ride a mere 1000 miles and write and publish a book about it. Sounds easy enough but I lacked the grit. The pages of the site are dotted with riders who set off from exotic places and have not been heard of since and I was now 66 years old and my biggest claim to fame was four days around Dartmoor in 2011.

When I set off that felt scary enough and nothing happened to me or the horse at all. So riding across Mongolia or through Africa or across the Carpathian Mountains was not really an option, least of all because I wanted to take my own horse and also I have suffered from an annoying UV allergy all my life that caused my skin to blister and swell, once on a ride through the Alpujarras region of Spain, where it was not even sunny. I ended up horseless and stuck up a mountain, awaiting a doctor to tell me that my microwaved, blistered face was in fact photodermatitis. So organised group riding holidays for me are not an option.

I have nevertheless managed to ride in several different countries and states; Iceland and Spain, Arizona and Argentina, California and Colorado and Tenerife . But apart from Arizona where I rode in a small group from Tucson to the Mexican border on a wonderful gaited Appaloosa horse that held the lead but accelerated when someone rode up behind him thereby preventing me from chatting to anyone for a whole week most of the rest were mere day or two day rides. I had my face wrapped against the soaring UV, resembling Katherine Hepburn in the African Queen but it still found the gaps and nuked me.

Still, having read as many Equestrian travel books about long-distance rides as I could from my armchair (figure of speaking I never actually sit down, except to write this book), I decided it was time to come out of the comfort zone and swing into the saddle. This time it had to be my own saddle and my own horse.

I have been to France many times throughout my life and arriving in Cherbourg never felt all that exotic, but this trip had a whole other feeling about it as I was ready to achieve my long cherished dream of riding my own horse on foreign soil. It was made even more poignant by the fact that in 2016 before I had achieved my mission with him, Salvador almost left this world after a battle with a very severe bout of colic.The vet had to pump out gallons of fluid in his swollen, distended gut and he was really ill. Made worse for me by the fact I was in Spain at the time, unsure if he would make it through the night, I sat in my hotel room on the top floor overlooking the city of Barcelona, powerless to act, just praying and chanting for a miracle. It was a long, anxious night. The vet went up at 8 the next morning and said he couldn't actually believe it? Salvador was up and eating hay. However against the odds and I firmly believe through the power of prayer and a miracle he pulled through and after a night on the brink between life and death, got to his feet and started eating hay. God must have saved him for a reason and that was when I made the vow to myself, if not now then when?

My relief and joy were profound and it was then I decided to stop procrastinating and do the ride I had been talking about doing for years now. God had saved him for me and I had to get on with following my dream of riding my horse abroad.

So I was very excited to arrive in France. All the dogs were barking below and car alarms were going off on the lower decks of the boat but my little Romanian, fluffy, rescue mutt Hunter was asleep unperturbed on the back seat. I hoped

9

he would follow us on foot and be a good companion to me and Salvador who was following with a mountain of paperwork (bad enough pre- Brexit, unfathomable now), behind me en route from Dover in a transporter's lorry. It felt amazing to be free of my responsibilities back home, it was just me and the dog those first couple of days.

We were heading down to Limoges in South West France to meet up with a woman, also called Ruth, who I had arranged through Facebook to ride with for the first few days. Salvador was to be dropped off at her smallholding in Meuzac . I thought I had plenty of time on my hands till he would arrive and Hunter and I were enjoying a wander around beautiful, historic Saumur, home of the elite Cadre Noir school of Equestrianism on the River Loire, when I got the call to say Salvador would be arriving in Limoges at 5pm and we were still about 4 hours drive away ourselves. It was then when I realised that horse lorries aren't as slow as I thought!

Panic set in and I put my foot down and arrived with our host just a few hours before the massive truck driven by a slender young woman arrived on time up the tiny road to the farm in the middle of a forest. He was here. It was real. For the first couple of days I hoped to let him settle in. The sun was strong by day and there were lots of flies, even horseflies, whereas in the UK not a fly is yet to be seen at this time of year. I was so busy congratulating myself on arriving and happy staying in the caravan in the garden along with the free ranging dogs, chickens and even a pig, that to be honest, that might have been enough for me. I could have stayed there, ridden around the local forest, achieved my dream of riding on foreign soil and gone home again to my other three horses in Devon.

But actually it was fear talking. I recognised the same feeling of trepidation I felt before I set off on the four day Dartmoor ride and had it not been for the hurry of my new friend Ruth to get off I might not have left so soon. We wanted to ride to Rocamadour, an incredible mediaeval village perched on a jagged rock face, straight out of a fairy tale.

I came to see that France has these kinds of jaw dropping places of unbelievable beauty ten a penny, particularly around the Dordogne and the Lot, although Rocamadour is something else indeed.

Ruth was a funny, chatty woman of many different talents. She is quite a bit younger than me in her early forties, an intrepid rider with a sense of adventure, a Northern sense of humour and she is also incredibly beautiful, of which she seems unaware, an Anglo-Indian with a great figure and a winning smile . She spent the next week in a battered cowboy hat and jeans and together we forged a friendship based on a shared sense of mission that will always stay with me. The morning we set out I first headed to Decathlon in Limoges where I bought a small tent, a stove, a sleeping bag lining and a few other items of camping paraphernalia . Ruth was under time pressure as she had only a few days to be able to leave her young son Milo with his Dad.

The previous day we had gone for a test ride but without any kit, my first ride on my own boy in France. Getting back from Decathlon with the gear I then actually had to pack it all on the horse for the first time, a jigsaw puzzle of balance but we finally got off and away with Salvador and Ted, Ruth's black and white gyspy cob, and Hunter keen to go, starting on a trail immediately opposite the farm in the mid afternoon sun. Salvador was carrying me, the tent and the camping mat rolled up behind the saddle, with a canvas saddle bag with two pouches where I had packed five days of food. I was hoping we'd find shops-after all this was France not Montana- a collapsible water bucket, (an absolute joke as Salvador wouldn't entertain drinking from it and the handle broke the first day out), Hunter's folding water bowl and food, maps, a portable stove, a tiny grooming kit and sponge, a hoof pick, a torch, my plate, bowl and cup, a meagre selection of clean underwear and cosmetics, a towel and a tea towel, washing up liquid, soap, first aid kit and two small bottles of wine one red, one white and as much fresh water as I could carry. A various selection of ropes were wound around the saddle horn and there were a lot of carabiners stashed everywhere. I cannot overemphasize the usefulness of these humble items, they attach everything to everything else. I also had a small backpack that I hated wearing but it carried my urgent supplies and a chunky fanny pack that contained my most essential daily objects; phone, passport, money, credit cards and reading glasses!

Never have I felt so free as I did then riding in the late afternoon sun in a new country with Hunter trotting along beside us. Already exhausted by the effort of packing up in such a way that meant my horse could actually move and I had a space to sit unencumbered as well as able to mount and dismount easily, we rode just 1km that afternoon before stopping to visit some friends of Ruth and got served a very British afternoon tea by very British people in a very beautiful garden, where the horses grazed around the orchard. When the friends offered us to stay the night there, I have to say we were tempted but dignity overtook and we swung back, well more scrambled into the saddles and set off again.

We managed only another 2 kms on some chemins and a couple of small lanes on my fat and slow horse that first day before seeing a hamlet where Ruth knew a lady with stables and here we stopped, untacked and unpacked, everything already covered in white hair from a suddenly moulting horse and spent our first night.

I spent the night in the half built guest annex, it had concrete floors and no furniture apart from one bed, thankfully and electricity. Ruth got a tent in the garden. We intended an early start but packing took forever, as it did most subsequent days and set off on busy roads but soon left them for the trail where we breakfasted on ham and goats cheese with a few oatcakes bought from the UK. I had a flask of hot water for coffee. We would try to ride a couple of hours before breakfast and stopped to graze the horses every two hours. Spring was already so established here in this part of France that thankfully we needed to carry no feed for the horses as wherever we stopped they were able to fill up on lush grass or Alfalfa, or the green shoots of other crops, getting plenty of herbs from the trail edges or roadside.

We rode 13 miles that first day down through Haute Vienne and into the glorious Correze, a region of the Limousin. We rode past herds and herds of the fabled Limousin cows, many with stocky calves at foot sometimes startled out of their pastoral lives by us and often very curious.

At the end of a long trek that day we arrived in the village of St Pardoux about 4.30 pm and to my excitement there was a bar! But alas, it was closed. We were to stay in the garden of Felix and Mary, someone Ruth knew, another schlep out of the village. Felix had been described as grumpy but when he turned up with cold gin and tonics and crisps he was not only actually quite charming but a Saint. Saint Felix? I never saw Mary.

Dinner consisted of horrible pale pink tinned sausages and Uncle Ben's rice but it might have been a Michelin starred restaurant meal, so hungry, drunk and elated was I. We camped on very prickly ground, and it was absolutely freezing that night. Eventually with the help of my herbal sleeping tablets I fell into a short sleep on what felt like a bed of nails.

We had tethered the horses to large trees. This was the first and last time I tethered Salvador as he woke me up at 7am crashing about with his hind legs tangled. From that point on I used my makeshift hi-line, strung between trees, this gave him freedom to move and lay down and gave me more peace of mind.

The previous night's euphoria had turned into tiredness by the morning and the horses too were lying down and I didnt want to make Salvador get up, as I figured he was tired after his lorry journey. I wanted to start easy with him and build up his fitness and stamina so packing up that next day was a slow task meaning we left St Pardoux later than hoped. By now I had started to crave my croissant or a french stick, purchased from the boulangerie that I figured we would pass if not today then in the next few days, or a coffee in a cafe, and it was tempting to go back to St Pardoux but we were already the side of the village on the route out and couldn't face that long trek up the hill once again but figured we could save it for another day.

We rode along quiet country lanes through pretty hamlets taking frequent, lush grazing stops. The weather was warm and windy with an occasional gust of chilly air. It was like winter and summer were fighting each other to prevail but luckily summer won. It meant taking on and off layers constantly. We started out in coats and hats and gloves and buffs and ended up by the lunchtime stop by the glorious old bridge of Vigeois, so hot that we and the horses had to dip in the river Vezere to cool down. It was hard to describe the elation of finding that glorious, ancient, riverside meadow with its huge shady oak trees to which I attached Salvador, beset with swarms of flies within minutes. Hunter grabbed the shade under the picnic table which he always did from then on when he saw one.

Our packs and saddles were strewn all over the place. We had a routine that on our tea breaks of say anything up to 30 mins we would leave the horses tacked up but just take bridles off to graze, at that point Salvador was still wearing a bit, but I came to ride him bitless in the end, but for our lunch break of anything over an hour we would completely untack. I had a Western saddle, light by Western saddle standards, about 25lbs, but still big to share a tent with it, and Hunter, although the latter slept on the numnah and sheepskin pad so it kind of doubled as his bed.

It was still and silent and we allowed ourselves a two hour lunch break here only interrupted by the town drunk who came down and asked to sit on Ted.

We tacked up again and rode over the ancient cobbled bridge into town. We tied the horses to the trees in the marketplace. Hooray, not only was there a bar but more importantly it was open. We sat down at a table in the most glorious square of the most glorious town and waited to place our order.

Why is it that the most idyllic looking towns can turn out to be the most grumpy and unfriendly type of places? The peeved bar owner who obviously found customers, particularly non local ones, a total interruption to whatever he was engaged in, watching a rerun of a football match perhaps, came out and grudgingly took our order making clear that the effort of listening to French with a foreign accent was too hard for him.

However the last laugh was on me as I had spied what the next table were drinking and I pointed at a chilled pink concoction and at that moment I discovered a Monaco, a refreshing mix of beer and grenadine. He had the next laugh though when we asked if he had food? His eyes rolled in despair at our cheek. Luckily we had eaten back at the river.

Hot, tired and a bit drunk again we thankfully only had a couple of miles further to go to our pre-booked destination for the night, a campsite out of town and steeply uphill, owned by Dutch people, therefore clean and well managed, friends of Ruth with a herd of magnificent gypsy cobs with flowing locks and with a proper field for our horses. Ted would have liked to join his tribe but he had to be content with Salvador that night just looking over wistfully at the elegant vanners. I slept so well knowing that the horses were enclosed and there could be no drunks or wild animals marauding. That came later!

It was so nice and organised there that we decided to take a rest day although we had only been riding two days and there was no actual rest.

I did my laundry and trimmed Salvador's feet. The long riding was wearing the toes but not the quarters (sides) of the hooves. Ruth's husband brought her son down to stay with us and so I was able to grab a lift back to pick up my car which I was bringing down the trail step by step when I could go and pick it up. A funny thing was that I felt this false sense of security having my car with me after living for the past couple of days with barely anything, except what was in my saddle bags, and my horse and dog. But when I had my car I had loads of stuff in the boot and it was nice to touch base with my possessions, I felt like I had a whole life back again. It's amazing how little stuff we really need as opposed to how much we actually have.

I charged my phone, always the thing that was in the foremost of my mind as a phone is so central to a long ride, being a communicator with the world outside as well as a compass, a GPS, a research tool for guide books, history and horse accommodation and a lot more besides.

Before I came to France I had a vision of a gentle day's riding from village to village, stocking up at shops and finding gites or inns to stay at with places to put the horses. The reality was completely different. We would often arrive somewhere after a long day's ride only to find that nothing was open- and hadn't been for years in some cases- and no one could or would put us up. After this secure little sojourn at the campsite we headed off into the wilderness, finding no shops and no boulangeries and no enclosures for the horses, so it was lucky that I went to the Intermarche in Uzerches and stocked up on supplies before leaving, only falling foul of the cashier for breaking French Etiquette because I broke into my hot roast potatoes in the store, whilst queuing at the butchery. I had to be contrite whilst she huffed and puffed, wiping the oil off her conveyor belt. I stopped again on the way back to the campsite at Mr Not Very Friendly's bar for another Monaco-no stopping me on this drink now. I should add by the time I left France I never wanted to touch grenadine again but for now it was my go to refreshment. It was a good day of getting sorted out for what was to come next.

We were accompanied out from the campsite by our Dutch friends on their gypsy cobs to the trailhead of the GR 46. GR stands for Grande Randonnee and is a network of hiking and if you're lucky, riding trails, across the huge country that is France.

It's a misnomer to call them trails because sometimes they are and sometimes they just go down country lanes and sometimes even alongside big main roads so you need a traffic -proof horse and a well trained dog to follow at heel. Hunter was not that. A Romanian rescue with a look of a dainty corgi, a bit of Pomeranian, the shouting fussy, fluffy bit, and a load of other breeds making a short legged, long backed foxy looking little creature.At 11 kilos he was a bit too heavy to carry in a backpack and he would have been indignant had I tried. Refusing even to wear a fluorescent vest, he trotted along the mostly quiet lanes but getting out of the way of an oncoming car was beneath him. He would just sit in the road and wait for a car to go around him. It is why I took him for the first week but eventually decided to leave him with family in the UK when I eventually went down the GR 65 the Pilgrims trail later in the year.

Another long day's trek took us through varied terrain and it was only once our friends on the gypsy cobs left us that I realised I had forgotten to buy the map in Intermarche.

Although I carried a selection of maps the only ones you really needed on the day were the blue maps, the equivalents of our Ordnance Survey maps, that covered the local area of the department and you bought those in the supermarkets of the place where you already were which seemed an arse about face kind of a French thing of which there were many throughout my stay. I have a good sense of direction, but without the map showing the chemins, the local footpaths and byways, you will be lost and have to stick to the lanes and signposts which may incur much more mileage.

Fortuitously at Bois de Contal, a grand sounding place but in reality only one closed up house, we met Carlos, a motorbiker equipped with a map who directed us.

Hunter had two scrapes that day. Firstly he took a deviation from the track onto one which ran parallel to ours but whereas our's started to climb his went down the road and we watched him get further and further away down the road, yelping as he tried to scramble up the thick overgrowth between the track and the road. Finally he emerged back on the track covered in spikes and thorns.

The second scare was as we passed a property with four big dogs on the GR 46, one broke through the fencing and bit him. Again he was yelping. Luckily he is so furry that it didnt penetrate the skin.

There are some horrible dogs in France. They don't seem to get walked much and some are hunting dogs that get out only in the hunting season, a hot under the collar topic that I will talk about when I got further South and came into contact with La Chasse. So it was a constant peril riding through France and at the very least dogs would suddenly bark and shock the horses.

After another long, hot and leisurely lunch break at a lake on a deserted property we had a short afternoon's ride into a place called Estivaux where we asked a nice man about camping and he sent us in the direction of the municipal campsite, another bucolic spot out of a children's fairy tale. I couldn't believe such an idyllic place existed, never mind that we could camp in it.

After allowing the horses some liberal grazing in the meadow whilst we put up our tents, Salvador was tethered to the hi- line and Ted to a tree nearby. We settled down by our campfire and had a great conversation about shamans and life, cooked a meal and had just gone to bed at about 10pm and I was drifting off into a dreamy sleep when I heard the sound of noisy vehicles approaching.

What came next was pretty scary. A convoy of battered vans descended to the river meadow and with their headlights blazing and started emitting, through huge speakers, the loudest, most hardcore techno music that continued all night but not before a guy who was obviously the leader of the group walked over. I was out of my tent by now and I told him about the horses, but he just said in broken English and I thought with some menace," You go, move ze horses now"!

For fuck sake! We were in the middle of nowhere, with no phone signal, we were tired. In the end the lesser risk seemed to be to stay put and hope these people would ignore us rather than pack up and head back into the depths of the forest at midnight. I felt a little soothed by the presence of a young woman in her own van who seemed halfway normal and tried to calm the guy down when she came and parked directly next to us.

Still I spent the night on tenterhooks worrying about poor Salvador the first night on his hi -line having to listen to banging music. Sleep eluded me totally and I was in a cold sweat in my tent until they quietened down some time into the early hours when just relieved we were still all alive, I grabbed a wink or two.

I was woken early by Salvador's shuffling to graze. I noticed as the trip went on how the horses stood quiet the whole night then they would start to look for grazing around dawn and I wonder if this is what horses do when left without humans around at night?

We couldn't leave the meadow quick enough that morning but not before we traipsed through the motley collection of battered, painted vans where the occupants now lay silently making as much noise as possible, determined to exact revenge for their disturbance. In any event no one stirred and probably wouldn't at any time in the near future. so with relief after only two hours sleep, we got off on the route only to miss the turning and had to double back on ourselves, climbing a steep hill in error where one of my D rings on my saddle snapped at the top. It took hours to get out of Estivaux. No one knew where the GR46 was and we had almost given up, thinking we'd have to go via the road when at last we found it. We followed that trail many miles that day in great heat and luckily it was well marked and took us through some stunning scenery at one point descending into a gorge and then up a grandiose, rocky promontory too humbly named La Roche rather than perhaps La Petite Montagne?

At a shady lunch stop I repaired all my kit, the useless and impractical water bucket and repacked my pack which was annoying me, slipping to one side and my tent likewise.

We rode seven hours on that day, the 7th of May. The terrain was stony, even rocky in parts but the trail once found and as long as we were vigilant was well marked. The horses were getting fitter and Salvador already looked absolutely amazing, having lost his English flab.

The next day felt long, hot and a bit tedious apart from the delightful surprise of riding into a town where there was a busy car boot sale in full swing. It was not so much the goods on display that tempted us, as we were not able to fit one more thing in our packs, although Salvador was kindly presented with what I used as a new saddle cloth/dog bed, a blanket with a cowboy design and a teddy bear on it but the revelation that there was fresh bread for sale. Alas as it was a public holiday it had to be pre-ordered and not even knowing where we were, let alone what date French holidays fell on, apart from that they seemed very frequent? Yet again we could not access the elusive boulangerie. Happily we were not entirely disappointed as a kind woman gave us half a warm, crusty pain de campagne and around a corner we discovered a stall selling burgers chips and beer. It was only 11am but beer and chips had never tasted so good. The kids made a fuss of the horses and Hunter slipped under the table of the burger man to rest and avoid the children who came to stroke him.

We 'parked' for lunch on a very dog pooped track up by the river where someone even offered us a cafetiere of fresh coffee for which I went to a gorgeous old house in Saint Viance town to get it whilst Ruth watched the horses.

The scare at the municipal campground of Estivaux had now faded into the recesses of my mind with the warm sun on my back and the blue sky and we hoped for a more peaceful night which eventually we found a few miles outside the village of Le Saillant. It was touch and go again for a bit but fate smiled on us again that night. We rode to the local campsite, a private one this time, absolutely idyllic, but this time in a French rather than Dutch way so things just lay as they were in a rustic kind of a way. We had to wait an hour on tenterhooks though as the proprietaires were out and we had read that you cannot camp with a horse on a French campsite. We hoped the owners had not read that rule! We decided just to speak to the owners nicely where I poured out our tale of two Anglaises riding through La Belle France. It worked . The night we passed there was as much heaven as the hell of the night before with Madame La Proprietaire stroking the horses enthusiastically and proposing us an oeuf or two from her hens for our supper and Monsieur letting us put our tack in the barn and charge our phones.

The final joy of that night was coming across the guests in the gite who plied us with beer and wine at their evening ritual of Apero which basically involves getting pissed and eating French cheesy wotsits and olives with friends before dinner and it is still to me one of the best French customs ever.

After a great night's sleep, a hot shower and with a fully charged phone we set off again into the unknown. We had been on the trail for six days now and with the exception of the car boot crowds and the drug fueled ravers, seen more cows than people and covered just short of 100 kms.

You think you will travel 25 kms a day every day but the reality is that's easier on foot, without a horse who has to take frequent stops to eat and remove or reposition packs and gear. The going was often slow and rugged or we often had to deviate via the road.

That last day's ride was no exception. The afternoon brought more roads and lost trail markers and I had to spend a lot of it on foot with Salvador and Hunter on a lead to keep him safe from the juggernauts hurtling past. We had to go 4.5kms around rather than the 1.5 km of the trail so when we arrived in the square of the town of Varetz, we were absolutely shattered. It was nice to be offered a glass of grenadine sirop and cool water and a bowl of water for a very hot and panting Hunter by a group of people sitting outside one of the houses.

Trying to find a place to camp that night was like trying to get blood out of a stone. Our enquiries yielded nothing and in the end Madame la Maire had to be summoned. She said we could camp at the municipal sportsground which was a little bit of a trek out of town. She instructed one of her minions in the assembled group of people where we had now had our photos taken and been interviewed for the local rag in the square to take us. Hunter meanwhile had decided he was going to live with these people. He didn't even care that his mistress was leaving. Eventually and reluctantly, still panting, he was bribed to come out from under the bench. It was now after 7 pm as we traipsed along the busy main road to Brive where we were installed unceremoniously in a sportsground, pitching our tents alongside a deep but not very wide river behind some tennis courts. Shortly after dropping us the man who escorted us came back with a bottle of Vin Rouge. I wish I liked red wine as I would not have had the perpetual dilemma of how to chill my white wine? But I don't, so I never quite got the pleasure of that first sip of cold, white wine as no matter how long it stood in the river to cool, it wasn't chilled.

I wanted nothing but to go to bed but we were being watched curiously by some men who played Boules well into the night and I could hear the noises of an invisible couple making out somewhere behind the trees and the rumble of trucks on the nearby main road. Overtiredness and anxiety kept me awake too long and I finally fell asleep but was then woken up and stayed awake for the rest of the long night by alarming plopping sounds which I thought were people night diving but I found out by daylight were giant water rats or coypu. They just drop off the river bank into the water. To add insult to injury we found out in the morning that Madame la Maire had not meant us to be taken to this sportsground at all but another quieter and prettier one on the other side of town with toilets and showers!

In the morning, well short of our goal of Rocamadour, having woefully underestimated how long the journey would actually take, not to mention the rocky terrain of the heart of the Causses du Quercy where it lay and with Ruth having to go back home, we sat feeling very emotional awaiting our separate trailer rides. Rather than negotiate the city of Brive and continue riding alone I had decided to cut out the 60 or so kms and get down to my next starting point and host in the Dordogne. I managed to blag a ride with a lovely lady with a trailer who came down from North of Limoges to drop me at the next leg of the ride. So here, in this unremarkable French sportsground as Ruth and I awaited our lifts and said our tearful goodbyes ended the first part of my adventure but I just wanted nothing more than to go on.

CHAPTER 2

THE DORDOGNE

My raison d'etre for being in far flung South West France with my horse was the trail riding there. Having ridden many a summer on Dartmoor, some warm, some wet and windy, some just plain old freezing, I craved new horizons and better weather. This has always been my Achilles heel, the fact that I get bored staying in one place. However beautiful others might perceive that place to be, I am a restless, nomadic soul. I love to explore new places. As lovely as parts of England, Wales, Scotland and even Ireland are, I longed to leave the familiar, yet damp, chilly shores of the UK. But I had horses and horses make you stay put. Yet I needed to travel. But how and where to? It had to be south for warmth. Getting to Spain seemed too difficult plus it's mostly quite rocky ground and my horse was unshod, as all my horses are and always will be, the reasons being too great to enumerate here but it's better for health not to bang nails in every few weeks.

Holland and Belgium seemed too cold and there's too much traffic on their roads and not enough open countryside. So in the end I chose France, because it was easier to reach with a horse and has a huge amount of quiet, open countryside and I even found to my delight that they mow the grass verges of every commune, meaning there's always a canter to be had anywhere. Plus I spoke good French.

I was lucky enough to have the perfect travel partner to carry me on the trip, a short and stocky Argentinian Criollo with a nifty turn, albeit often in the direction of his choice and pertaining to that wonderful equine term, "a leg in each corner". He was described as a roan on his passport but he was actually a bit spotted and a bit flecked. He was brown on his ears with a splodge of brown on his rear. Criollos, as I found out, when I went to buy him out of a field of about 50, are often interesting colours. He was stubborn as the mule that he resembled with his pink spotted muzzle and hooded eyelids that always needed a fly mask on or they'd become easily irritated, especially when it came to being caught or conversely stopping still to chat to someone en route whilst mounted when he became very restless and desperate to go on, whereas actually riding him when you wanted to he would sometimes barely go and occasionally would turn around without warning to go back home. But as soon as you mounted him you had to get that leg over quickly as he was off like a shot and a lack of rider agility would have you over the other side of the saddle in a ditch.

I guess a lot of these were just bad habits that the Gauchos in Argentina overlooked or even encouraged. I always felt he had a grudge against people. So I cut him some slack. With his unimaginable six week sea journey from Argentina to Italy, then a lorry to the UK, he must have been traumatised. On his passport photo he looked startled, muddy and forlorn like a refugee off the boat. It was a miracle he was so safe and steady and for this I adored him and tried to turn a blind eye to the fact he would not be caught until he had run a large circle around me, coming tauntingly near enough for me to reach out to him and at the last second before capture, set off smartly but not before he presented his rear and a hind leg to me, missing me by a calculated whisker. I figured if he'd have been really trying to hurt me he'd have double barrelled.

Taking food to bribe him didn't work either as he'd grab the food and run off. I always factored in extra time to catch him so he could first show me I couldn't catch him before eventually he decided I could and would submit to the halter.

Even wearing a field safe headcollar,(never leave an unbreakable halter on a horse by the way) did not help, unless I attached a bit of extra rope to the buckle under the chin when he became a lamb to catch. Once caught he was an absolute gentleman. I just figured he enjoyed showing me that he was the leader in this game. It had to be a mental strategy I used with him as he was no psychologist.

When I got him in 2005 he was called Figo meaning Fig but that seemed a very feeble name for such a stoic warrior and so I renamed him El Salvador which literally means the saviour and he became mine. Were it not for him I would not have been riding the wooded chemins (countryside tracks) of South Western France, nor experiencing the absolute thrill of riding in the sunshine in another country, but might be still trotting over cavaletti in an arena. Not that Salvador would have enjoyed that. Salvador does not jump. He looks like he should, being compact with a powerful rear end but he just couldn't see the point in elevation and when faced with an obstacle he either just crashed through it, or if too daunting, skirted around it. In fact he had no vertical movement at all other than as a protest when being asked to load in the small horsebox I bought and ultimately had to sell because eventually he wouldn't set foot in it at all.

I'm a firm believer that the horse determines the equestrian direction we take if we let it? But most people, rather than fit in with the talents of their horse, try to adapt the horse to their equestrian pursuits and therein lies untold stress and frustration.

For example, I used to love show jumping. As a young woman in my twenties I went off in my lorry to indoor jumping competitions. I had a super, mature, jumping pony born for the job but he couldn't do dressage and was too bouncy to hack out on. So to turn a horse into something it really doesn't have the penchant for is a waste of energy. Better to be an all round horse person and adapt your own goals to the horse. This is what I was doing with Salvador as he didn't care to go that much but preferred to go forward when he did, so off South we set.

So that morning on the outskirts of the city of Brive, in the Correze department of the Limousin, after Ruth and I parted company, Ann, the lady from North of Limoges dropped me an hour or so later, at the small but pretty village of Grolejac which basically was merely a crossroads, running along the magnificent River Dordogne on one side. There was a small supermarket, a boulangerie with tables outside, a proper restaurant, although I never saw anybody eating there, and a stand selling melons or whatever fruit was in season, a canoe rental business and a closed down garage.

However it was civilization to me and had a hotel, the Hotel du Pont. It was run by a couple, the friendly, front of house, Thai wife and he, the French, and not so friendly cook, husband. There was a terrace in front on which I drank many a Monaco and some pastis as well and even ate the pretty tasty menu du jour a couple of times in the old fashioned but ornate dining room. Grolejac is a one horse town and I had brought the horse!

Salvador and I were dropped at the house of Helen Edmonds, my next hostess, up a farm track a mile outside of the village but ascending steeply. It was lunchtime and my driver and I were liberally fed. Helen welcomed us with roast chicken and roast potatoes and all the trimmings. Although Helen was English, she had adopted French habits, this lunchtime at least. I love that about the French, how they stop to eat lunch. It's a part of their culture that they take seriously, everyone stops to have a cooked meal and a break. Unfortunately it is being eroded in favour of 'un sandwich', a generally butterless chunk of French bread filled with ham, cheese or sometimes vegetale which is basically just salad . You only get butter with your bread at breakfast and that's that! So if you ask for it with your bread at any other meal you are considered rather a misfit.

My horse and I were here but my car was still a couple of hours drive back at the Dutch campsite and since Ann, the lady with the trailer was passing pretty close by there on her return, I grabbed the opportunity and legged it back up with her to the Haute Vienne to collect it.

I left Salvador with the Edmonds, Helen a psychotherapist , her British West Indian husband Brent, a crime writer, and their two adorable little girls along with Helen's horse, Lincoln, an enormously fat white cob, a few dogs, cats, chickens and a goat.

Their fencing left something to be desired and I hoped Salvador would not escape whilst I was gone. Lincoln and him had a cursory sniff of each other but it looked like being buddies was not on the agenda. They pronounced each other uninteresting and Salvador tried in vain to find something nice to eat in the scrubby pasture.

Relief at reuniting with my car was once again strong and even Hunter seemed happy to have his back seat back to himself again. The drive back down again to the Dordogne, twice in a day on that same route, was tiring. Luckily French motorways are mostly empty, especially outside of July and August, the holiday months.

The Astra had started making a rather loud squealing noise when I braked which stressed me a bit. Cars are beyond my comprehension and despite a lifetime of having them I can still only guess at what's wrong, although I'm often right? I thought maybe the brake pads needed changing. But also on this drive down an error code on the dashboard illuminated saying code 84 which when I looked it up in the manual, simply said engine power reduced. This according to Astra geeks-what a waste of precious life energy I figure it must be to be one- could have many causes. Taking it to a dealer was the consensus.

So I knew I would need to go to a French garage post-haste. Helen suggested her mechanic Franck, pronounced Fronk, but sitting waiting for him to come off the phone in basically a graveyard of ancient, broken cars, you see it a lot in France, I was not too optimistic. My Astra was not new , a 2011 plate but it looked very posh here. It turned out he was about to close for an extended holiday weekend of which there are no shortages in France . He shrugged but was not forthcoming. Again luckily for me, or so I thought at the time, although there's no Vauxhall in France, the Opel Astra is essentially the same vehicle. There was an Opel dealer in nearby Sarlat, a charming mediaeval town in the Dordogne, its only downside perhaps is that there's one too many an English person there. It's cringeworthy to sit next to these pompous Dordognophiles, overhearing their loud conversations in the local restaurants as they know it all about France, about the food, about the weather and even about the politics .

Yet these are the people who also whine when they can't get cheddar cheese or 'proper' bacon or sausages or Bisto gravy. They attend sell out fish and chip and curry nights put on by the local expat community and they rescue cats and dogs, only the latter action being of course to their credit.

May and June bring the most fabulous weather in South West France, yet campsites and hotels lay empty. The French, unlike the British, find it inconceivable to vacation any time other than the two most sweltering, uncomfortable and crowded months when they swarm down to the idyllic areas and coasts. It was good for me though.

I was pleased to get back to Helen's where the plan was to ride on with her through the Dordogne. I would get my car fixed and spend the next few weeks riding, appreciating the beauty of the Dordogne . Helen had been an enthusiastic supporter of my dream and had even organised a Facebook page for the ride.

I had lots of offers of support and accommodation en route and in fact all over South Western France. The page became a great resource for my information and planning. I made many contacts for all stages of the ride.

I was very excited that she had offered me grazing and accomodation and a chance to explore this beautiful region and that was why I came here because when you are riding long distance you need some safe anchor points on your trail.

Helen and Brent very kindly gave me their bedroom in their quaint, higgledy piggledy stone home. It was indeed a hobbit house. However they had neither enough grazing nor accommodation for me so it was arranged that me, Salvador and Lincoln would go to a French friend of Helens, Briacca who had a safe enclosed paddock and a spare room.

The next morning Helen took me to visit Domme, a mediaeval bastide village high up overlooking the snaking River Dordogne. It was straight out of Rapunzel. I was enchanted. It was then that I decided I had to stay in this area at least for a while. I wanted to find a house of my own here.

Briaccas house was a bungalow surrounded by a hectare of paddock on the bend of a busy road and people would speed round the bend and toot and wave. Fortunately it was secure and well fenced, a rare thing in France, where most equestrian land lies within a tangle of electric fencing, although there was no shade. It was now early June and suddenly the days were very hot. Briacca was very helpful, she took Hunter to be clipped for me and kept her eye on the horses. Riding had to be done early in the morning as it was already sweltering by ten.

Helen and Brent had a million friends and contacts and Helen seemed to be a very busy woman. Although she would come to ride those first days I was there, it tailed off and I actually started to feel a sense of chaos around her which made me feel a bit vulnerable, as I had come to hers to join with her for the next leg of my ride, but she could barely find the time to ride Lincoln. She was also worried about her weight and decided she might walk rather than ride on the next leg.

I moved into Briacca's for a few days which made me happy to be living with my horse but it was a brief respite as Briacca smoked instead of eating, a tendency which I think may be common in French women of a certain age. It was not just that she smoked but was a chain smoker and everywhere indoors. The pungent, sickening fug of smoke permeated every room of the house, even the bathroom and I just felt nauseous and after retching in the sink early one morning, whilst cleaning my teeth, I knew I would have to leave there quickly. At the same time Lincoln and Salvador had grazed the paddock bare and were still not getting on that well.

Helen had a French neighbour who had a large house which was often empty, they lived elsewhere, far away, as do many French people and only used it for holidays and she arranged with the neighbour that I could stay there. It was a beautiful house from the outside but a cold,dark, functional and not very comfortable place with a million shutters that I had to keep opening and closing when I went out. In the end I left them all closed and just lived in one bedroom with an electric heater left on. The good thing is it was only across the lane from Helen's. I tried to make myself at home there but I didn't really like being alone in a big,empty house.

Before I came Helen had told me that she had plenty of grazing for my horse. What I didn't realise was that this grazing was not actually hers. Not only was it not her land, it belonged to farmers she didn't even know and involved going into literally the middle of nowhere, based on pinpointing a pen on an ordnance survey map, miles from where I was now staying, with no people around and staking a claim on a parcel of completely wild land with no vehicular access nor water for the most part, with electric fencing posts and tape.

We rode miles from where she or I were living to get there. I tried to write my phone number on Salvador's rump with an indelible marker but it soon rubbed off.

I couldn't really relax or sleep at night thinking that my horse might escape onto a road or even be stolen or maimed. There had been spates of horse abuse and violation in France and I was not comfortable with this arrangement.

Meanwhile I had to do something about the squeal and the error code on the car. I went to the garage in Sarlat where I painstakingly explained in French-my French was good but became much better by the end- including boasting an in-depth vocabulary of car parts, and spent the whole day wandering around the quaint and touristy city of Sarlat, breakfasting in one cafe, followed by eating a plat du jour at midday, France's answer to an express business lunch, except you drink wine and eat for longer, followed by lots of walking, discovering the ancient streets, markets and parks, culminating with a drink in a cute bar, I went in for a cup of tea but the people on the next table had something cold that looked nice so I ordered 'le meme' (same as them).

Finally it was 6.30, the time garages close for the day in France having closed for hours over lunch. I called them as instructed. The car was ready! Hooray! I duly paid the bill for the computer fault reader, and the error code removal.

They had identified the cause to be the Solenoid which they had replaced. It was 500 euros.

I drove back to the house that evening feeling a lot poorer but relieved. The light was off but the brake noise was still annoyingly there.

Meanwhile Helen's behaviour became more and more erratic. She would arrange to ride or meet but was frequently terribly late and constantly let me down on arrangements of all kinds, especially the one to ride together. It just never happened. She said she had to work every day yet never mentioned it before I arrived. Not only did we only manage one more small ride together but she couldn't even cope with looking after her own horse now he was in the wilderness. We had to drop off heavy plastic containers of water that became too warm under the hot sun. If I hadn't gone and done it would she have just left them in the middle of the forest to look after themselves I wonder? I couldn't imagine how she ever thought she would be able to go off on a long distance ride.

She was always trying to loan him to someone else to ride too. Had I known all these things beforehand I probably wouldn't have come but the saving grace was the immense beauty of the Dordogne and being able to ride there, albeit mainly alone.

I felt very stuck now as the weather had become too hot and I had no horse transport and I also needed to get back to the UK to see my family, particularly my aging parents who I felt responsible for if they needed me? The plan had been that Helen would look after my animals whilst I went back home for a couple of weeks. But it soon became apparent that I would not trust her to do this.

Helen was a complex character, lovable, yet highly manipulative. She never slept, banging out emails in the middle of the night and was completely chaotic around arrangements. There were definitely money issues too, although things were offered abundantly, I actually felt like a cash cow to her. She offered so much which felt unconditional yet was it all really with an ulterior motive? I don't know but I felt that Helen had concocted a plan in her mind ostensibly in offering to care for Salvador whilst I went home but which was actually for me to leave Salvador with her for one of her daughters and other summer visitors to ride out with her. Being a bit ditzy was one thing but actually I feared for her mental health. I now wonder if she may have been bi-polar? Either way, as kind and intelligent as she was, I felt very trapped, ironically by the total lack of structure.

It was time for me to move on, I urgently needed to go. But how, with no transport and it was too hot to continue riding without a base? And where to? I called the number of a guy I was given by Ruth, a mate of hers, who amongst other things drives ancient Land Rovers to France for Anglophiles who love ancient Land Rovers. I arranged with him to bring my 4 x 4 Toyota and trailer from my home back in Devon. He was brilliant. My truck got its MOT the same day I called, thanks to my lodger who took it to the garage and it arrived in the Dordogne two days later. I can't describe the relief I felt at reuniting with my Land Cruiser and having a way out of there. But now I had two cars and a trailer to deal with as well as a dog and a horse!

Luckily throughout that time in the Dordogne nothing adverse happened to the horses and poor Salvador seemed oblivious that his safety was on the line.

I told Helen I had to go, citing my need to keep moving on with my ride, which was true. I had met a couple of horsey British women nearby through my Facebook page and we met for coffee and croissants at the cafe at the crossroads in Grolejac. They both shared the same surname Brumby, but were not sisters as I had first assumed, but bosom buddies. One of them arranged to board Salvador at their farm and I would go to stay at a campsite by a lake in Gourdon, the nearest town.

Leaving the lonely house was a stressful affair. Helen had not even mentioned money during my time there but when it came time to leave she asked me to pay her 100 euros in cash to give to the owner. She was the master of springing surprises upon you at the last minute. I closed the massive house up for the last time at the end of May 2018 with relief, but great difficulty, as none of the locks worked properly. Helen broke the key when she came to check and got into a wrangle with the owner about it trying to blame me for her heavy handedness. I was not sorry to exit the Dordogne.

That was one bright and beautiful end of May morning that dawned when I rode the few miles into the Lot, physically close but psychologically far away. That ride felt liberating and heavenly.

The Brumby 'sister' that was having Salvador, Margie, walked with her sons to greet me at the entrance to their village and accompanied me on foot all the way to their home. I felt like a hero. But she was my heroine as she enabled me to leave an increasingly challenging situation. She drove me to get my truck and trailer which I parked at their house. What followed was a wonderful week exploring the amazing trails and scenery of the Lot.

I spent one night in my tent on the campsite by the pretty lake when the heavens opened up. Cold, sodden and wet, I moved into one of the empty gites where I spent the following seven days before finally leaving for that visit home to the UK.

Every day that week I rode out with my new friend on her black and white gypsy cob Oscar. The scenery and landscape of the Lot was as stunning as it had been in the Dordogne yet more open and a bit less quaint. Over every hill a vista opened up then there were forests and chemins and quiet country lanes. I could now relax after my time in Dordogne where I was constantly on tenterhooks. I was also able to leave Salvador and Hunter with the Brumby family for 3 weeks and travel back to the UK to see my husband and family.

I know I haven't mentioned my husband yet but it's a long story and it's not what this book is about. But in the summer of 2015 I married a Zimbabwean musician whom I met in a small Devon town in 1999. I was very much in love back then you could say besotted but it went wrong and it was on and off, mostly off, over the next ten years. We were now reconciled and got married and had a cosy home life together but I couldn't let a man stop my mission. Also we had long talked about leaving the UK to settle somewhere warmer in Europe, so we saw it as a reccy. He was a pretty self-sufficient kind of guy. As long as he had beer, his mobile phone, a guitar and something to smoke, he barely noticed I was gone. In the end his marriage to alcohol caused the breakup of my marriage but that's another tale. I still love him or more precisely fancy him, which at the age of 70 is not assured. But love is not everything as in the end you have to be compatible. I should have left him in

Zimbabwe and gone for a fling every so often instead of breaking myself in two to get him legally to the UK. For what? They say absence makes the heart grow fonder and so far we've been apart for 5 years so it's probably more that absence makes you forget the bad bits. I haven't had the heart to divorce him so far, and I'm unlikely to want to marry again. We are still in touch.

I drove to Limoges airport again up that same motorway past all the places we had ridden through, an hour long drive, a week long ride, where I left my car. It squealed all the way to the airport and just before I got there the error code light came on again.

I went to England and tried to forget about it. When I got back to exit the airport car park I tried to pay the parking fee which was 64 euros. But the machine wouldn't accept credit cards and the attendant was at lunch. So I went to an office in the tiny airport and the guy just let me out for free. This is one of the things I love about France, its human side. When technology causes a problem they sort it with a shrug.

Back at The Brumby's, both Salvador and Hunter were fine, Hunter having taken over the couch of one of the Brumby's dogs. Plus it was now deep into June and hot as hell.

Luckily it was still not tourist season and my gite with a view over the lake was still available. I rode in the mornings with Margie and we shared some natural horsemanship techniques then I went back to the campsite at Gourdon at night where I found a mechanic who had 'Les plaquettes de frein', brake pads, written on a big sign outside his workshop. I assumed this meant that fitting new brake pads was an everyday experience and what customers might in fact come for? Not so. After another long explanation in French not receiving any credit from them for being able to discuss the mechanics of brakes, no less in fine detail, they managed to persuade me that the pads were not worn but just had dust and dirt in them. I was sceptical but they know best, right?

It was whilst sitting on the pretty terrace of the hotel in town, drinking coffee in the shade and once again waiting for my car to be fixed, that I received a call from Helen saying that she was going to delete my 'Ride through South West France' page now that I was no longer 'at hers.' I was really surprised and shocked, asking her why she needed to remove it as it was a useful resource with so many contacts and interested people all over the region? Her rationale was that she had set it up for me but now I was no longer under her wing so to speak, she didn't see the need to continue it. I asked her to please wait until I could get all the contacts of the people and all the pics of our riding to date off of the page and set up my own page.

Within the hour the page and all its messages, communications and images were deleted. All of the history and pictures and record of my ride vanished into cyberspace. I was gutted. She blamed her friend who had been "messing about" with her computer and supposedly deleted it by accident!

I will never know if she was telling the truth or was just plain vindictive. I doubt she would even admit it herself. Either way I blocked her on Facebook, the only time I have ever done such an act and have never spoken to her since.

I had been asking around for a livery somewhere safe where I could base Salvador for the heat of the summer and hopefully head back to the UK again in August where I had more official things to sort out and a husband who I thought would need reminding of my existence. The idea of going for a long ride over weeks, months or even years doesn't take into account-at least for me- that it cannot be a continuous thing as you have to account for weather that is too challenging to ride in, or that you have to attend to aspects of your life beyond the ride that won't wait. I felt vulnerable with no next place to wait out the summer heat.

By a stroke of supreme luck a barefoot hoof trimmer friend of mine saw my post and told me that her sister and mother had a farm in the Gers down to the far Southwest just below Europe's largest pine forest, Les Landes. Not only that but Bex suggested I might also like an air conditioned mobile home thrown in too? I couldn't get there quick enough.

CHAPTER 3

THE GERS

I arrived in the Gers, department 32 on Sunday 10th June 2018, with Salvador in tow. In the event what Google maps said was a 3 hour drive took me over 5. I guess Google France figures French drivers are more reckless than a 66 year old English woman towing her horse through France. I went safely and steadily and it took forever, but my faith in my own abilities increased when we made it. I'd decided the best time to drive would be on a Sunday morning when lorries were absent and the roads were quiet, as people were either at church, hunting or getting drunk-in some cases all three- but hopefully not behind the wheel on the major roads. The quaint vistas of the Lot opened up into long distance horizons in the Gers and we passed fields and fields of vines and ripening sunflowers.

What greeted me at the lieu dit Caillaubert, (place known as....), the quaint way in which French country properties are often addressed, was a huge farm of 100 acres inhabited by only five horses, mostly, in fact completely, unrideable 'field ornaments' that had no expense spared in feeds nor medicines to keep them alive by their doting owners. They received 24/7 nursing care and Salvador, breaking the pattern, being both healthy and rideable, would be welcome to join them at 300 euros a month.

This was an answer to my prayer as I needed somewhere to go and somewhere to leave him in good hands whilst I went back to England again to see my husband and family and escape the heat. Thanks to this timely response to my plea for help from my friend on Facebook, I was able to bring Salvador to this stunning farm where I was also able to rent a capacious mobile home situated in the huge horse barn so that I could be close by my horses all the time. It even had Air Conditioning.

My ride had to be held in check for the moment due to the increasing heat, so I was happy to have found the perfect place to wait it out. I got out on Salvador in the early mornings before the flies appeared, including some monsters with green unforgiving eyes and such on the lookout for easy blood, especially if you go exploring Gascony as I did.

It's quite wild countryside although very agricultural. There are grapes and sunflowers and loads of maize, the cobs of which Salvador learned to hone straight into and artfully snack on liberally whilst en route. There's big, open vistas and you had to ride through people's fields at least around the edges. There didn't seem to be any bridleways at this point but the great thing is that these huge fields mostly all had tracks around the edges allowing for long canters.

Some mornings on the more remote farms across the other side of the N124, the main trunk road that went from Spain to the Landes, we would see a family of wild boar trundling through the maize, the mother sow followed by lots and lots of tiny little hairy boarlets. Astonishing to behold and I became heartbroken by the awful attitude the French have to sanglier. It is very difficult to oppose the rural attitudes

44

to hunting or La Chasse as it is grandly called. It is considered to be part of the fabric of French rural life when the great estate holders of the French empire and their peasants unite over their lust for blood. In general British people in France are divided into two camps. Those that have the mindset that it's not their country so they can't oppose tradition, which approach I find ludicrous as if you have moved to live somewhere, albeit you are not a national, you still have a right to an opinion and do not need to put up or shut up and those that are vehemently anti-hunting, like me, although I didn't properly live in France and to be honest probably never would due in fact to their great attachment to hunting. It is not like the UK where hunting is illegal but people still do it anyway and the worst that can happen is you get some snotty whipper-in on a rather out of control horse telling you they are following a trail when the hounds are miles away on someone's land baying for blood. No! In France it is quite possible that you or your pets will be maimed or even killed by drunken, marauding countrymen with guns on your Sunday morning stroll through the woods.

Apart from this aspect I absolutely adore France, especially from a riding point of view. At this point I didn't want to go back to live in the U.K. and certainly didn't want to take Salvador back. He looked and felt so well as did I and Hunter who'd been shorn again for the heat. The only downside was that I missed my family and friends. Especially as it was in the mid 30's most days and it was a long wait till it would cool down enough to go riding properly again.

I had now been in France for six weeks and the hardest thing I had to deal with was myself. Once it became impossible to continue moving south on horseback I found myself on my own with Hunter, my only companion in a mobile home. Even if I rose early and squeezed in a fly-free ride around 5.30 am, this just left a long, hot day with nothing to do. I spent long periods of time with me, myself and I and of course Hunter and the horses but the lack of companionship depressed me.

This is not a state I aspire to, being a do-er rather than a be-er and I really don't know if I'll ever really relish long periods of being on my own? But I had no choice but to wait it out till it cooled down sufficiently before I could get back on the trail again.

But I absolutely adored Caillaubert, a magnificent, colonial, Gascon Farmhouse with a palm tree outside the front door looking something like a diplomat's villa in the tropics rather than a house in rural South West France. It's hard to describe the beauty of the sunsets over the stunted but iconic Mediterranean pine tree, home to an army of processionary caterpillars. Processionary caterpillars are accepted and dealt with by locals but seem to be the bane of English people, who I suspect are rather scared of these features of Southern France's buzzing insect life, even getting somewhat hysterical about them regarding their spiky hairs that dogs can get harmed by . Certainly in all my time in France, even running through the woods, my dog never got involved with them but I guess some dogs are not so lucky or sensible.

The summer slowly passed and autumn approached. One day I crossed the lane outside the farm and looked over the fields and there to my absolute shock and surprise appeared a white topped mountain range in the distance only visible several months after I had been living on the farm. It was faint but nevertheless I recognised the iconic vista as the Pyrenees. They had been there all the time and I had literally had no idea.

This was another thing that made me want to stay there. The idea that the Pyrenees were accessible, albeit about a two hour drive, opened it up as a great place to live with skiing, hiking and climbing possibilities.

I went to the garage my landlady used and recommended. It was run by a rather young and handsome mechanic, the son of the owner. Although quite a smart looking garage, it still had the obligatory row of ancient Renault 5's and 2CV's that were no doubt hopefully waiting for their turn to be restored to their former selves at some point in the future which seems to be never.

I explained to Gabriel about the squealing and the error code and he told me to jump in whilst he road tested it. He then proceeded to drive my Astra at breakneck speed along the N324 for a few miles. It was white knuckle terrifying. I just wanted to jump out. The car handled perfectly, no squeal and no light, making me feel like an idiot as you always do when you take cars with inexplicable problems to the garage and they don't do the thing they do with you, but then on the last bend before the garage entrance, the brakes squealed and the error code light came on simultaneously.

Gabriel was short on explanation but convinced he knew what the problem was. I was less sure he knew but I was instructed to return it the next day where I duly left the keys with an elderly man behind the reception on the phone who could not stop coughing. I had to wait ages for him to come off the call listening to his hacking cough. It was pre- Covid so I assume it must have been cancer or emphysema.

The man was part of the generation of French people who find it hard to listen to French spoken by a foreigner, screwing up his face with the pain of listening yet then talking to me at such speed in a heavy Gersoise accent, that I literally could not understand a word. I just nodded and left the keys with him coughing his guts out and hoped they would actually fix it.

The next day I received a call from Gabriel to come and collect my car. Hooray the squeal was no more and the error light was out. Another 500 euros was duly paid to Gabriel via the coughing man.

There was no point in trying to ride and the days were long, hot and boring. Salvador was in the safest of hands so I decided it was better to be in the UK for a couple of weeks and visit and trim my other horses, see my family and sort my affairs there. I flew back to the UK for 3 weeks this time and then I went back again in August. I had reached the end of the road with the Astra, although the brake pads were changed and the squeal gone, the error code came back on with a vengeance. I decided I would have to get it back to the UK as the problem was not going to go away here. Registering or selling a foreign car is almost impossible in France and it's just easier to buy one there. The drive in August back to the UK was frustrating, the error light came on at every bend all the way up France. I stayed the night with Ruth as I drove up the same old motorway through the places we had ridden past. I had to stop at Arnac Pompadour too, the grandly named and stunningly beautiful centre of French equestrianism named after Madame de Pompadour, a favourite of King Louis XV, housing the glorious National stud and Anglo Arabian breeding centre, to get Hunter vetted and treated for tapeworm, which was a requirement of dog travel in 2018. But I got to the port and on the ferry eventually. It was still so easy in those pre-Covid, pre Brexit days to get back and forth.

I took the Astra into a garage near my parents home in Wantage, Oxfordshire. They fixed it for £39.99. A loose wire had been shorting when dislodged-hence the bends-rendering all talk of hundreds of euros to fix it null and void.

However there was too much water under the bridge. The Astra and I were still not on speaking terms and I left it in the UK with my son to sell.

I was very lucky my mum had decided her BMW series 5 was too big for her to drive and they had bought a smaller car. The incentive for her was that her garage was being demolished to build an annex and my parents don't like their cars being out. So on that next trip out, the BMW was to its surprise, as it was not really familiar with animals and nature, stocked up in its huge boot with bags of horse feed and packets of dog food and horse rugs and then it purred its way down to the Gers, with Hunter on the floor behind the driver's seat. What a relief to drive a lovely vehicle that although not new, had lived in a garage and done about ten miles since it was bought. It may not have been my exact choice of car and I hated the fact that I was obviously going to incrementally ruin it but I was so grateful to have it and be rid of the Astra once and for all although it was actually behaving perfectly once it was back in the UK.

I arrived back in the Gers on the 1st September 2018. It was still hot but the intense heat of August had abated .

49

Back at Caillaubert it was now time to think about the next leg of the ride again. When I moved down to the Gers I had no idea that the famed Pilgrims Trail or Chemin St Jacques, the Compostela way, went through the Gers passing a mere 5 miles from the farm. It is a well trodden route on foot, Pilgrims yomp miles daily from spring to autumn, staying on the trail in communal gites and hotels or camping. I got used to seeing the many hikers walking through the neighbouring towns and villages, sometimes along the main road and past Gabriels garage. You would see them, young and old, from all corners of the world hanging out or having a coffee in the tiny town or villages at the cafe in the square in Eauze, sometimes sunning themselves in shorts and T shorts and at others soaking wet, covered in plastic rain sheets, including their backpacks from head to toe . They were pilgrims walking the Pilgrims trail or the Chemin as it is commonly called on their way to Santiago de Compostela in Spain.

Sometimes you would see scallop shells stuck on walls or posts or painted on the road and this I came to discover was the emblem of the fabled St Jacques way or Pilgrims trail or via Podensis, or in our riders speak the GR65. It was during this long hot summer, whilst walking Hunter one day, that I saw a marker on a tree that said GR65. The huge numbers of hikers with large backpacks, the people draped in pac-a-macs from head to toe sitting in the squares of some of the towns I visited, it now all started to make sense.

Once I realised that the trail almost passed my door I became quite fascinated to find the access points nearby and I was like a dog with a bone. I walked and drove around the area with my Pilgrims trail map that I found in a bookstore in Vic Fezensac hatching the next plan- To ride the famed Pilgrims trail.

CHAPTER 4

THE CHEMIN ST JACQUES

The Pilgrims trail or Chemin Saint Jacques, Santiago to Compostela in Spanish is less well trodden by horse riders than hikers. I arranged to ride this next leg with Vicki Drury, an English woman who lived in the Lot in France and did endurance riding. Vicki and I had been talking for many months about riding a trail together and she had wanted to join me at the outset but because of her endurance riding season her calendar was booked up until September.

When I told her I had realised I was based only a few kilometers from the Pilgrims trail she said she would join me on my ride down on her Connemara gelding, Mouse. The plan was for her husband Barry to accompany us driving the truck and trailer carrying electric fencing posts and tape to make corrals, as Mouse would not stand quietly on a hi-line like Salvador.

She agreed to come down to the Gers with horse Mouse and husband Barry-Baz- who would drive a support vehicle to meet us every evening with tents, electric fencing and more importantly food.

Liaising with Baz was quite tricky as he could only access the trail at certain points where it met the road, so communication was paramount if we were not to waste precious time setting up camp in the evenings. Baz would also reccy places to stay ahead of our arrival and transport the camping gear and food. He would do shopping en route and brought his electric bicycle for him to potter around on waiting for us to arrive. This would leave us free to ride more distance carrying only day packs, and nothing heavy, hence we'd be free to have a canter here and there.

We set out on 6th September in sweltering, albeit less sweltering, heat than July, from Manciet, ironically starting right opposite Gabriels garage, where we intended to ride a distance of around 200 kms to St Jean Pied de Port in the Pyrenees where the Compostela nears Spain.

Vicki, Barry and Mouse arrived the evening before, September 5th, and spent a cramped and fairly sleepless night in the other bedroom in my mobile home before we set out on the trail later the next day. A twisty ride took us to the start of the trail at Manciet. I photographed the marker gleefully. We were on the Pilgrims trail! The trail started around the edge of a maize field and went right through the middle so we were immediately able to have a lovely canter.

The daypacks were bouncing around a bit as we cantered through the field. We rode into a massive area of vines and tracked between them onto a lightly wooded track, past a fantastic horse farm with a tree house. I didn't know at the time that it was a livery yard that I would later approach to board my horses in. We emerged from this track at a stunning ancient chapel with a Maltese cross, called l'eglise-hopital Sainte-Christie sitting in a glorious meadow of wild flowers.

Here was our first day's lunch stop. We untacked and propped the saddles up on a tree and took the horses to graze in the meadow. We left them untethered as they were

53

grazing so peacefully, side by side, when a single fly landed on Mouse and he started to move. Salvador, who barely ever moves when grazing, decided to set off too. Vicki lunged for Mouse but it was too late. Within an instant they were gone, back off down the track and into the vines. Our chasing after them was futile. They had vanished. Mouse was still in his bridle and Salvador in his headcollar and there was no sign of them. At that moment I had a choice to panic or not to panic and just have faith that we would retrieve them in one piece and I chose the latter as it just seemed too mad and big and hopeless to panic about.

We had made our first big and stupid mistake not tying them up and as we berated ourselves we tried to think as horses and went to the horse farm, but they had not gone that way and the horses there were grazing quietly obviously unaware of any local escapees. Luckily we were still not far from the starting point, precisely 10kms and I was able to call my landlady who said she would come in her Land Rover and grab us and go to the chapel, which fortunately had a vehicle access point, to collect our gear. There was nothing for it but to set off on foot retracing our steps to meet her on the road . It had now also started to rain. As we breathlessly trekked back to the start point through the vines and maize, there on the ground to my astonishment lay my long tethering rope that had been clipped on to the horn of my Western saddle.

My rope is such a critical piece of kit that if we had not had to retrace our steps, I would have only discovered it was gone too late. I cannot imagine being without it on the trail.

Back at the road I met an old man driving past who slowed down and asked in French, "Are you looking for some horses?" I said yes and he gesticulated that they had just gone through Espas and were headed up to the main road.

Again luckily, as my landlady left to come and find us, she saw the horses heading up the road towards the farm and quickly phoned her partner, who although not a horse person by any means was instructed to stand in the road and block the way to the main road to Spain, a mere few hundred metres past the farm, with his arms out like the aeroplanes he serviced for a living. It worked. Mouse turned into the farm from where we had started out that morning with Salvador following 15 minutes later-as I said he is lazy- both having travelled the 10kms back home. Neither horse had a scrape on him nor seemed any the worse for wear. Mouse had only spent one night at the farm yet his homing instinct was impeccable. And all because of a bloody fly!

There was nothing to do with the rest of that day but open a bottle of wine and have an early night back in the mobile home and prepare to do it all again the next day.

So on the 7th of September we set off again on the real start, and passing the site of yesterday's debacle early and without hitch, got to Nogaro for lunch where we stopped on the outskirts of the town for a picnic lunch under a shady oak at the bottom of someone's garden, who kindly came and offered us water. Through the centre of town we rode, past the bank and cinema and up the steep hill out of town before deviating off onto the trail again into the countryside and made it to Arblade le Haut, looking for accommodation by mid afternoon. But not only was there no room at the inn, there was not even an inn, nor anywhere to stop and rest up. The tiny village seemed to be empty-we found out later from Barry that we had not actually reached the village proper which was a bit off the trail- so we had to continue on. We then hit the very busy main road, the N324 and rode with the trucks from Spain roaring past and then just at the last minute before entering Lanne- Soubiran, the trail deviated to the left. It suddenly became quiet and rural again. As we approached the hamlet of Lanne -Soubiran in the low early evening sunshine there was an ancient Gascon homestead with a house and some small, typically Gascon, timbered barns. By now tired and erring on the side of panic that we would not find accommodation -a theme that repeated itself again and again on the ride-we knocked on the door and asked the owner if we could put up for the night in the field with our horses in our tents? To our relief he said yes but then we had to go and find Baz with the trailer and all our worldly goods. Baz was parked further along the trail at the biggest maize farm imaginable, having already gone for an electric bike ride, so we had to go back and forth .

Salvador set to work snacking. The farmer came out and chastised him for nibbling his cobs. Surely he couldn't miss one or two cobs in this enormous plantation?
"It'll kill him ", said the farmer.
Makes you wonder what the hell they are putting on it if that's the case?
Back again to the field, we immediately set to work installing two corrals for the horses with electric fencing.

This was always the first thing we had to do on this leg of the journey as Mouse was far too frisky and full of himself to be tied to a tree or a line. Even though he was 25, he was the most energetic Connemara with a lot of attitude and spirit. I adored his attitude and his owner Vicki has had so many wonderful endurance rides with him. It took ages and by the time we got around to putting up our own tents we were a bit fractious and just wanted to go to bed. Vicki and Barry are Yorkshire people that don't seem to tire of baked beans, but I have to admit I just longed for a prix-fixe somewhere or a menu du jour. But baked beans it was.

A glass of chilled white wine might have redeemed the situation but as I said earlier, no matter how cold the stream you stand the bottle in is, nothing equates to white wine out of the fridge. It still has that effect on the taste that it is more sour and fiery than chilled white. Especially those tiny bottles you put in your saddlebag. Plus it doesn't really go that well with baked beans!

I cannot remember if I slept that night and I probably didn't as I hardly did on the trail. But whilst we were packing up the camp we saw walkers coming past us with their big backpacks and sticks and realised that the place we had just stayed was in fact an official pilgrims' Gite and we could have had a bed or even a cottage for the night. When we went to pay up the owner showed us around the place equipped to sleep for 30 people. Instead of having to beat my way through overgrowth to find somewhere to poo, I could have just used the toilet.

Swinging back into the saddle and off at a steady walk, we watched the Pyrenees grow closer, at first as a distant mystical range that began to loom large as we headed down through many villages and tiny hamlets on the route, steadily growing in stature as we headed South West. Baz did such a valiant job in the support vehicle, carting electric fencing and feed from one place to the next. This was not made easy by the fact that we had no idea where we were going to stay on any night? It was a matter of luck, some more so than others and it was a pain erecting a corral at the end of each day and dismantling it in the morning, as well as having to set up a fresh human camp daily.

That day, Saturday, we followed the trail through some delightful villages and in one,Lelin -Lapujolle, we found a cafe serving a delicious salad of the day with bacon and toasted walnuts, served with an ice cold glass of Perrier, whilst the horses were tied under the shade of a tree in the village orchard, resplendent with tomatoes and apricots and apples lying on the ground.

We were aiming for a fairly sizable town that night called Aire sur l'Adour as it had a campsite which we thought it might be possible to camp in?

But by late afternoon after riding a long, long, stoney track alongside massive maize fields we actually arrived exhaustedly at a place called Barcelonne du Gers.
It was as far removed from its namesake Barcelona as could possibly be, however it had a tabac, a shop and a hotel. We felt we could go no further that day.
However our enquiries yielded no suitable places to stay.

After wasting time enquiring to the owner of the hotel about accommodation, we could have had a bunk room but Baz would not share and anyway there was no place nearby for the horses to stay, it was now getting late, the sun was setting and we felt we had no choice but to ride on towards Aire sur l'adour.

Just as we headed out of town, past the church where Mouse deposited a massive croc,(poop) a sign to the right pointed to a recreation ground. We ventured in to look, and here, past the tennis courts at the bottom end of the car park were some picnic tables and some allotments with more tomatoes and pumpkins and an almost enclosed little area of grass. We would only need to enclose a bit of the area as it had fencing to 3 sides and there was a toilet in the car park too so we decided to put up for the night here. It seemed the best option under the circumstances.

Having corralled the horses by the allotments, I walked back into town. As large as it was, it had no open bar, only a tabac and pharmacy. On investigation the shop was not really a village shop as such but a growers cooperative that sold an eclectic mix of organic courgettes, smoked salmon and beer. I bought all 3.

Back at the makeshift campsite Vicki had flooded the bathroom, the tap wouldn't turn off, and Baz was cooking for us, if it can be called cooking, a dinner of Fray Bentos tinned stewed steak, tinned potatoes and tinned peas.

It was a cooler evening and although I cannot say I slept like a log, I did relax and awoke to a morning of light rain which meant putting on all our rain gear but then having to remove it almost as soon again after, as the sun appeared in the sky clearing to another hot day. Salvador was stepping out really well as we headed out of Barcelonne du Gers and off we jogged over pavements and roads and zebra crossings over a grand bridge into the pretty town of Aire sur l'Adour, blessed with early autumn sunshine, which in actuality had only been a few minutes ride further on.

We had to ride right through the centre of the busy town, passing shops, bakeries and cafes but being Sunday they were all shut. The only thing that remained open was the ATM machine that we rode past and where I dismounted to get some cash out. People were not used to seeing horses in the town centre and on the way out I dropped my torch,another essential piece of kit, and had to get off to pick it up prompting a passer by to ask me if I had fallen off?

It was a steep, steep climb out of town past some glorious, if rather faded, mansions and gardens, some modest bungalows and even huge derelict looking religious buildings. We were blessed at the top of the trudge with a nice grassy field where we let the puffing horses recoup their energy with a juicy graze.

A few kilometres outside of Aire sur l'Adour appeared a surprise, a gorgeous recreational area called Lac du Brousseau that we lunched at and rode through.
The peak of that day that started out cool and rainy was by now boiling. We stopped for a break at what looked like a bus shelter but I could not imagine a bus appearing in such a remote area. According to a nice man we met, who had walked from Le Puy way above Lyon, it was a pilgrim's shelter from the heat and dust. We all had lunch in there including the horses who took the opportunity to hide their heads in the shade of the shelter.

Another very long day's trek again culminating in an endless track, brought us to the village of Miramont Sensacq-there are some lovely names in this region- on the edge of the Basque country.

Thank heavens for the Gite communal. Here we booked in with Mary, and were soon installed in our corral and tents in the camping field behind the Gite. Not only that, but we were able to charge our phones in the Gite and even get a hot shower which was bliss.

We had been asked if we wanted to join in the communal meal for 10 euros but said no. This was a decision we lived to regret as it smelt so delicious.

But we even got ice from the Gite and so the wine was cold and a delicious accompaniment to the gluten-free pasta and sauce I made myself for dinner.

Baz and Vicki were having a heated discussion about something, as married couples so often do, so I retired early to the sanctuary of my own tent. I didn't sleep a wink that night, There was no reason for sleep to elude me. There were no plopping coypus, or shagging couples or heavy traffic in fact no sound at all.

The trail was getting steeper and more winding. The flat maize fields gave way to hills and long climbs. We managed a 9 kilometre trek that morning to a midday lunch stop at Pimbo.

Pimbo is a glorious bastide village, with an ancient church, a pretty cafe and a gift shop with a menu outside, adjacent to the tourist office selling tea towels, with shady tables and stunted trees to which we hitched the horses.

But what appeared to be the self-imposed guardian of the village, a middle aged woman came out to yell at us. She said we were rude not asking if we could tie the horses to the trees and moreover if the horses were to deposit a croton, which Mouse already had, there would be hell to pay.

We apologised profusely and asked may we tie the horses up here? She said yes but tutted and scowled.

We hoped to bring peace to the one occupant of the deserted village by going into her cafe/shop for lunch. I asked her what was the plat du jour (dish of the day)? She answered me in French, there isn't one. "Il n'y a pas de pain." There's no bread.

Ok I enquired undaunted, " Qu'est ce qu'il ya à manger ?" What is there to eat? She answered, still scowling, "Rien" Nothing.

I know that French people in villages can be traditional but surely the lack of bread need not also cancel out all food?

We made do with a packet cake and a coffee. The woman didn't crack even a hint of a smile when we paid and left.

There was some jubilation for us when we returned to the horses and saw both boys had deposited massive turds by their respective trees. Tempted to leave it as a gift for Madame we decided to kick it about and cover it in dust and rode out of Pimbo like outlaws.

A long, hot afternoon's ride brought us into Arzacq-Arraziguet, a fairly sizable town, to the Pilgrims Gite, a sizable hostel, right in the centre of the town. This one was marked by a sign and busy with pilgrims, washing their socks and relaxing. I had called and booked this one ahead and they said it was ok for two horses to camp but looking at the place I couldn't conceive of horses staying right in the centre of the town like this?

What a surprise then when the receptionist led us through the complex of buildings that made up the Gite into a central courtyard and out under an arch into the garden. Here at the bottom of the garden was a small area of paddock where we were instructed to erect our fencing.

This is what I love about France: it can be so unpredictable and beauty is all around even in urban areas.

Dinner was a disaster for Vicki and Barry that evening. Having missed the set meal that smelt delicious the night before, we booked the dinner here. But it was a rather tough roast duck leg which neither of them would eat so the chef made them a fried egg. They complained and grumbled all the way through the meal where we sat at a long table of mostly French pilgrims but with a few foreigners. I attempted to chat to some of them but Vicki and Barry were fed up.

The saving grace was that there was a bar next door to the hostel and I managed to get Vicki to accompany me for a chilled glass or two of white wine where we pored over the map and discussed the next step.

On Tuesday the 11th September, five days' ride down the Pilgrims trail from Manciet, up high in the beautiful Bearn, after passing a large group of unfit looking but friendly German hikers puffing up to the top of a steep path, we accidentally deviated from the trail. No amount of backtracking or map studying could find where we had lost it and how to find it again?

For some reason I had decided to prioritise style over function on this part of the ride. I was wearing a riding skirt made of gabardine that I had had made up for me by a dressmaker from my own pattern. I'd had an idea to promote and sell them under my equestrian wear brand, Equestrian Nomad. My mission was to bring back romance and even a dollop of glamour into riding wear which I felt had become very masculine particularly in English riding.

Whilst the skirt, which is basically a pair of long, wide culottes, was waterproof and could even double as a cape that covered the rear of the saddle, it was extremely sweaty to ride in here. I was combusting with heat and had lost my stirrup tread, so was riding unevenly with different leg lengths. We were on the edge of a village named Fichous-Riumayou that was not on our map and there was a network of D roads crossing the edge of the village.

We really did not know which way to go? On top of this there was absolutely no phone signal to call Barry and let him know.

There was nothing for it but to stop, untack and have a long lunch and rest in a very awkward spot on rough ground as we would obviously have a long afternoon to rectify our route. A French lady hiking alone passed by looking for her daughter, a pilgrim. She too had lost the path.

Eventually after skirting around on the road for a good distance, we relocated the trail. By about 5 pm we arrived in the charming village of Larreule. Stopping at a bench by a chapel we just felt we couldn't go on any further that day. We were frazzled.

Luckily two bars of phone signal popped up, enough to Google the village and see there was a Gite that accepted horses. It even had a proper paddock for the horses and a swimming pool. I called and was told cheerily yes come along.

Imagine our surprise when we saw the Germans all laying on turquoise towels on sun loungers around the pool. And they had got there long before us by the looks of it.

Patricia ran a very busy gite and chambre d'hotes. No sooner had we arrived than a large party of French guests arrived on foot with a load of luggage delivered in a minivan.

The horses were turned out freely into an idyllic paddock with post and rail fencing and a palm tree.

We put up our tents as far away from the other guests as we dared. It was stonkingly hot still even at 7pm. As I pegged my tent poor Baz just fell out of the truck and collapsed into a heap on the ground. It looked like he had gone into a coma. After a little while he came around shakily. But the heat and effort of towing the vehicle had been too much and he had underlying health conditions anyway. Luckily after a rest and some cold water he perked up and within about 30 minutes was shouting at Vicki again.

In the dining room the meal again smelt fabulous and we were sorry we had declined to partake but when we actually saw it was roti de veau, relieved. Vicki is a vegetarian and I don't eat baby animals, very hypocritical I know, as Patricia and her husband were obviously seriously good cooks which makes sense when you are running a chambre d'hotes I guess.

The place made some cash selling cold drinks from a fridge on the trail that passed by the road on which the gite sat. I bought lots of bottles of cold water and a couple of organic blonde lagers to accompany the baked beans now Baz had revived.

The next morning with no fencing to dismantle and a long trail still ahead of us we intended to leave early and beat the heat. But it was still 9.15 am by the time we hit the trail outside but we soon made Pomps where we had been hoping to stop the previous night. Thank goodness we hadn't made it that far, as the pilgrims' Gite was not nice, very institutional looking and concrete.

The village had a small pilgrims' shop, an epicerie, where the lady shopkeeper had to be summoned by a bell. There was not much in the shop, but there was the fresh fruit that I craved. I bought peaches and grapes and two cooked sausages that turned out to be gritty and tasteless. Vicki got seriously ripped off by the lady and when we realised what she had been charged for a few measly items we spent the whole of the rest of the morning complaining about it. We were besieged by flies and had to swat them continually.

It was on the long afternoon's ride into Arthez de Bearn that Vicki caused us to really fall foul of French etiquette again.

It was a simple enough proposition. We passed a tap with a hose attached on the side of someone's barn at the outer edge of a farmyard alongside the road on the last leg of the route into Arthez somewhere near the tiny hamlet of Mondi.

I suggested we ask if we could use it to draw water but there was nobody around. So Vicki decided anyway to hose down a very hot Mouse and at that moment a man drove into the farm and got out and started yelling at us.

He was absolutely livid and I was upset with Vicki for not understanding or caring how easily the French react to anyone not asking about the simplest things like using an outside tap or tying a horse to their tree. I felt she never listened and always tried to buck the system. However, spending a lot of time with someone you are bound to discover you have different ways of doing things and our differences abated as the depth of the bond strengthened as our ride progressed.

We finally rode into Arthez about 3pm, slogging up the last long road into the town only to be photographed as Pilgrims of the week by the local rag! Annoyingly, the communal Gite in town did not open until 4.30 pm so we could not pitch our tents or rest the horses. The streets were very narrow and there was nowhere suitable to park a 4 x4 and horse trailer.

Finally we were admitted into the Gite and instructed to take the horses and truck and trailer around the back via some very narrow roads. Frayed tempers ignited into a major conflict as the truck and trailer entered the camping field which was actually a steep orchard littered with ripe figs.

Baz struggled with getting the rig into place but wouldn't let Vicki drive it either. He became a crazed driver with the vehicle's wheels spinning and getting stuck. He hit bushes and ended up hurting his foot so badly that he couldn't walk up the steep steps to the showers in the lodge.

He was obviously reaching the end of his stamina, and I realise now, quite unwell and we were all tired and needed a rest.

It was a pretty town and an idyllic gite, especially down in the fig orchard, although better for donkeys or mules than horses one would imagine and it was rather hard to contain them on such a hill.

After a shower at the gite, Vicki and I decided to go out for a meal and left Baz there with his foot up and a meal of baked beans and his book.

As was so often in such towns there was to our dismay, no food and nothing to eat but thankfully there was a bar open serving cold white wine. Dinner that night consisted of wine and peanuts. I got drunk and collapsed into my bed.

It turned out to be my last supper on the Pilgrims trail. We woke up and abandoned the mission as Barry was in too much pain to go on. Unknown to us then he had broken his foot. He had been a valiant crew member but his health just couldn't take it any more.

It was hard getting the trailer out of that field and righted back onto the road out, Vicki had to drive because of Baz's foot but she gave it some welly and miraculously, as it was extremely narrow and muddy, out into the street it came. We had to load the horses up in the town square and Salvador was not impressed and didn't want to squeeze inside the jam packed trailer .

We finally set off out of Arthez heading North, with Vicki driving, me in the passenger seat and Barry grumbling in the back. But eventually he put his headphones in and silence reigned. It took 2 hours for Vicki to drive the overpacked truck and trailer back the 100 kms to our starting point at Cauillaubert.

After a quick tea break with Mouse back on board they set out for another 3 hour drive home. I was relieved to be back. Salvador was happy. I was happy. I slept 10 hours that night.

CHAPTER 5

THE SCRUFFY DOGS OF EAUZE

My local town Eauze (pronounced Ay-oze) was charming. I liked going there, especially on Thursdays, when there was a wonderful,weekly French market. I say wonderful, mainly it was the food that was wonderful but the other stalls, with a couple of exceptions, notably one selling bales of hay and straw, which I didn't need, but as a lifelong horsewoman, pleased me nonetheless, were fairly utilitarian and on the one occasion in my life I wanted to buy a large polyester tablecloth I was in luck!

Eauze was my nearest proper town. Eauze is a town with a hell of a lot of history including at one time being the capital of the Roman province of Novempopulania a few centuries ago and has a nice climate, albeit a tad too hot in July and August.

There are a couple of reasonable places to eat lunch, as long as you like confit duck and chips, including a nice cafe in the main street opposite the square and next to the Bank that feels very French and I could imagine this spot being the hub of Eauze life for hundreds of years.

I would not be the first nor the last to wax on about French markets; to describe the wonders of the produce, almost all of it locally produced. The cheeses, the breads and the fruit were something to marvel at. In the UK if we get one or two goat cheeses we think that's choice, but the market here had dozens of goat and sheep cheeses.

Shopping for food in France is as serious a business as eating. They don't really go for junk food, at least not the older people, but of course young French people love their Maccydees as much as young people anywhere the world over including in Asia where the local cuisines are, in my opinion, the best food anywhere.

There was a choice of cafes for coffee and sometimes I'd briefly meet a British acquaintance there. But in Eauze I was befriended by a gorgeous Algerian woman. We chatted in French and she bought me coffee. It made me feel like maybe I could make a life here after all?

Eauze is 130 kilometers from the Spanish border and a town on a main N124 route to the West.

Every week the road closes in barriered sections so that the most massive convoy of aeroplane wings can pass through on monster trucks from Toulouse. If you are either lucky or unlucky enough to get in its path, depending upon how much of an aeroplane geek you are, you would be truly gobsmacked by its size as it trundles along the route.

As you approach the town there's a busy roundabout and at that roundabout there was a large wood yard with a big workshop and here lived two of the hairiest, scruffiest, dogs ever seen. They were nonetheless very cute.

I would drive past them every time I went to town or up north. Sometimes they were in the yard but mostly they either laid in wait at the roundabout and occasionally would jump out and bark at a passing vehicle or were asleep on the edge of the road. They seemed very savvy despite their lack of grooming.

I often liked to go up North to Gondrin where I had a friend, or Condom, the butt of British jokes, which despite its rude name, actually pronounced 'Co-do' by the French, was a charming and pretty town, with nice cafes and restaurants and shops, not as far North as Agen, which felt completely different in character than the Gersoise towns and not as exotic as the towns lying in the Southern direction towards Toulouse or the Pyrenees. However its claim to fame was it had a train station with the TGV.

After the summer the tenants moved out of one of the gites on the farm and I moved into the Gite, a house with two bedrooms.

My landlady and her husband were a godsend. They were so kind and hospitable to me. I also made some nice friends, mainly British and although I was not technically single, my husband was absent enough both in body and mind for me to feel it was acceptable to join a group of single Brits for some social dinners which were fun. In any case there was not a chance of any romance in these groups which were as is the case world over, largely composed of single women. One of them, Judith, a pretty Welsh lady in her early sixties with great white teeth and winning smile, she had been a dental nurse back in Wales, became a good friend that I am still in touch with today.

I am not a good photographer so depicting the stunning beauty of this countryside was not my skill. I leave that to my son Silver Levy-So, a wildlife photographer whose enchanting images of his weeks sojourn in the Dordogne encapsulated the history, magic and and lusciousness of that region with its ducks and geese and truffles and gastronomy, not that I sampled too much of it as I didn't want my own 'foie gras' literally translated as fatty liver.

Lunch as I already said is sacrosanct especially in these rural parts of Gascony. I couldn't really adapt to this ritual as eating heavily and even worse, drinking 'du vin' at lunchtime meant wiping out the afternoon going into the evening and being a lightweight drinker I couldn't drink again the same day so I stuck with a cooked breakfast of eggs and veggies and coffee at lunchtime till an early dinner and a sensibly timed apero of a glass of wine or pastis or both sometimes with my landlady and her partner at 7pm, followed by dinner at home in my gite.

Apero is one of the best things about France to me. It is an extremely civilised ritual of wine and crisps or even a Pastis, tomate cinquante et un, basically a pastis not with tomato but with Grenadine and sometimes even olives or nuts and ham.

My ride on the chemin had come to a rather abrupt end, hastened by the ill health of Vicki's husband Baz. Had we known then what we know now about Covid and Brexit and the rest we would probably have kept going but it seemed a sensible decision to load up the box and pile in and drive back to my place in Eauze to take a break as a week long ride with all the gear in tow and having no booked places to stay at night and having to erect corrals and fencing and tents had taken it out of us a bit so it was easy to give up at that point in order to rethink the plan. But once back, rather than hang up the old riding boots, the long distance riding bug was still biting.

During the summer when it was so hot I had visited Lupiac and was breath taken by both its beauty and more relevant to me, its connection to D'Artagnan, who was actually Charles de Batz de Castelmore d'Artagnan fictionalised by Alexandre Dumas as D'Artagnan, one of the Three Musketeers. The reason being that he was a great horseman who these days sat still as a statue in the village square, surrounded by impeccably preserved, typical castelnau architecture. Being there felt like stepping into a fable.

The forest resting majestically outside this tiny place, deep in the middle of a quiet area of the Gers, was the starting point for lots of different riding routes which were grandiosely marked on a signpost in the town square, including even one to Paris and Maastricht in Holland, via Luxembourg. I imagined arriving triumphantly in Paris and riding through the Bois de Boulogne, possibly sidesaddle, back in the seventeenth century.`

I became besotted with this place with its historic square displaying the arrow and signposted the Route Royale, Paris pointing this way and Maastricht the other although surely at this point I would have thought both left Lupiac on the same trail? I couldn't imagine anything more exciting in my future than riding a horseback trail to Holland and I returned over and over to Lupiac, walking the dog around the magnificent lake at the start of the trail.

I went into the tourist office, amazingly it was open, and tried to convey my fascination with the idea of riding Salvador to Maastricht to the lady in there. When could I start, I wondered?

It turned out that Lupiac's grand statement is literally just that.

There is in fact no trail, just disparate trails all up the country that don't quite connect yet but hopefully at some point in the future they will. When and if that happens, then you'll be able to ride beyond the forest in Lupiac. Meanwhile it's just a gorgeous place and a great project.

That autumn 2018 was warm, stunning and mellow but a decision beckoned. I needed to go home as I had three other horses with a harsh winter on Dartmoor beckoning and no one to look after them.

But the idea of departing this gorgeous country and its mild weather for the rain and grey of Devon didn't appeal to me, and there and then, I made the decision to stay and bring over my two geldings Patriot and Warpaint. My mare Opal who's a tough old boot would be cared for by my neighbours.

On October 1st 2018 my two geldings arrived, none the worse for wear but a bit shaky and tired, just as Bex left with her 5 horses on the same lorry to return to the UK. And just like that I was alone at Caillaubert with my 3 horses.

I imagined Salvador would be delighted to have his yard mates back and all my boys together again. None of it. He was most upset that Bex and her horses left and was not at all impressed by Warpaint and Patriot despite having spent years living happily with them. He called and called for Bex's horses, none of whom had really seemed to like him much. Horses are funny creatures and their allegiances can change at the drop of a hat.

Eventually they all made up and things settled and I was over the moon to have my boys together on such a fine,fine yard.

My landlady, the owner of the farm, was not horsey and left me alone to manage the place and my horses as I saw fit. Both her daughters had now returned to the UK and she was not in good health. The farm was too much for her and she was also now desperate to sell the place and even offered me a swap of my Dartmoor farm with 18 acres for her French one of 100!

I sincerely contemplated it but unbelievably at that time the value of mine in the UK was more than the value of theirs, complete with colonial Gers farmhouse, manege, incredible barn and two cottages and 100 acres of grassland. But once swapped I would have been left with no cash to manage it. Also it was a seriously large place and I would have wanted to operate horsey and yoga retreats but it was quite isolated, far from an airport, and with an absence of public transport. As I said you would really have to go to Agen to pick up guests arriving by train or Toulouse 1.5 hours away-assuming the convoy wasn't coming through. In those pre-Covid days it was so much easier to get back to the UK, which I did frequently to see my family and stock up on essentials that I couldn't get in France, mainly for the animals. Despite the distance to the airport and the fact that it took around twelve hours by bus, although if you could get to Auch you could get the train into Toulouse and the airport bus, which I did a couple of times, I loved the ease of Toulouse airport and the fact there was never any much traffic through the Gers apart from the one night we had to wait for the convoy.

I did have some support out there too. In such situations as being in France, only a hop across the channel yet as foreign as they come to Brits, expats tend to stick together and even help each other more willingly and I met some horsey folk who were so helpful to me, especially the wife of a JCB diggerman, who came to help me with my horses a couple of times a week. I was quite nervous riding Warpaint out there. I don't know if it was the quality of grazing or just the new environment or the vibrant wildlife and nature out there, or the relentless killing of it, that got in his pants? But he was quite fresh and forward sometimes and I needed someone to come with me, so I felt safe, and that's what she did. Religiously walked at my side as I rode through the idyllic countryside and I can't thank her enough for that support. I also met up with other expats for meals and events, some of whom I really liked and some of whom I didn't rate so much.

It's a funny thing that as a Brit abroad you end up connecting with people you have nothing in common with and wouldn't pass the time of day with at home.
But despite all this the reality was, maybe because it is such a rural country, I felt lonely there, especially once Bex had left and in the end that was the main reason I didn't agree to the swap.

I made another quick trip back home on Halloween. On October 31st I went with the whole family to the magical national Westonbirt arboretum in Gloucestershire . The sun shone and I felt so happy to be with my kids, my sister and my parents and even my husband came and appeared to have fun.

The next morning I took my husband to Heathrow for his plane back to Zimbabwe. He was to make a 3 month trip home to see his family and escape the harshness of winter in Oxford. I was angry with him for going for 3 months even though I had left him to ride. Once he was there I told him it was over for me. I have not seen him since. I miss him sometimes. They say absence makes the heart grow fonder but it can also extinguish the flame. I still loved my husband, but even being away from him this time could not make the spark that I had once felt for him rekindle. I decided unsuccessfully to try to move on.

Perhaps it could not have ever really worked given the differences between us. My friend who is a Christian says that the bible says a couple has to be 'equally yoked'. I suppose it looked to him like the UK streets were paved with gold, compared to the commercial reality of high density, Harare suburbs where you might score an egg or a cigarette from a street vendor. But there is still an energy in Southern Africa that is missing in the UK.

I don't think that after the initial excitement of being here he felt at home and was often troubled by the idea of dying here away from his family and ancestors.

But ultimately it was not so much about money but behavioural differences. There was no way of scouting around it. My husband was a functioning alcoholic. Shortly after our wedding I went to bed as he was drinking beer. When I came downstairs at 1am he was in his vest drinking and dancing and conducting a monologue about how the world had yet to acknowledge his greatness.

I was, for the first time, scared of being in the house alone in the middle of the night with my new husband. He was never unpleasant to me or aggressive in any way but I just felt that he was so incoherent that it was scary.

In Zimbabwe people drink and it is not unusual to see someone in a pub holding their heads in their hands, so drunk that they are catatonic. It is a cultural difference as far as I can see. He comes from a country where men smoke and drink excessively and rather than a disorder, it is considered to be part of being a man. He said his father drank and smoked too.

I knew he liked a beer or two but in England he started drinking up to 5 or 6 large bottles of Heineken a night.

After the first couple he was engaging and charming and chatty, but by the fourth he was talking nonsense.

He was indeed an extremely gifted musician playing guitar and bass and he had played in bands both in Africa and the UK. At one point I had even managed the band, in the days when African bands were a novelty at any local festival and could command a fee.

But he was also quite anti-social and his favourite thing was playing and recording his music, track over track, originally into an old fashioned 4 track machine and eventually into a laptop.

He was not much of a foodie, unlike me, only eating to survive, which I suppose having been brought up in a poor family and society meant scarce food. But he smoked and drank like a fish.

The easy use of technology here was very appealing to him at first, having come from a country where there was barely any internet in the poor suburbs and even a phone call was distorted and got cut off frequently and you often ended up speaking to someone who wasn't the person you called. Shortly after our marriage I discovered -as he had barely concealed it-that he had been messaging young Phillipino women.

I was devastated and in a temper threw him out which he said made him feel desperate and scared. Maybe I overreacted? I don't know. I was a relatively new bride and even though he was unlikely to act out his fantasy on a 14 year old Asian girl, I felt hurt by it.

Somehow we managed to work through it though by him getting a job and us living separately and eventually I forgave him and I spent weekends with him at my house as he lived in a room with no bed, just a cover on the floor, as he didn't seem to care about comfort. Or I would just meet him in the city, have some drinks and food and go home again. This was much better for our relationship as I felt free when we just dated, even if I paid.

By 2017 we had done a lot of work on our relationship, or perhaps to say I had and maybe he had, and we were living back together and had moved from Devon into my apartment in Oxford, where it was easier for him to work, given he still hadn't yet passed his driving test. He could drive well but his driving could be erratic and obviously always was when he sat the test . But he was not really happy in the cold, damp of the UK and I can't say I blame him but it was never an option for me to go and live in Zimbabwe, although I think there would have been a lot of opportunity there to run a business together which is what we had always said we would do. I had visited Zimbabwe four times since 1999 when I first met him and the country was stunningly beautiful, yet terribly oppressed by Mugabe on all my visits there .

Back at Caillaubert the glorious French autumn faded into foggy November and then winter but it was short-lived and not bleak like UK winters. The days passed with me walking Hunter in the countryside or around one of the numerous lakes, stopping to drink a bitter coffee in a bar and eating too much stuff I shouldn't eat. like croissants and duck fritons, delicious crisp morsels of fried duck skin.

It was dry and I was able to ride and enjoyed some great rides on Salvador. But once I had done my horses and walked my dog the same issue of the long day stretched before me. Occasionally I looked forward to lunch with one of my friends or a coffee but mostly I did not have enough to do there.

I went back to the UK that December, where we had a big family gathering in Oxford and my landlady kindly looked after the dog, whilst Jo, the diggermans wife, came to do the horses. None of them even needed a rug that winter. It was so mild. I returned to France and spent Christmas Day there on my own.

Thankfully a friend, one of the ones I still like, invited me over for drinks and snacks to their family and my landlady and her husband cooked me, and the abandoned erstwhile son in law who was still there, bemused at why Vix had upped and left him without an explanation, a lovely roast for which I was so,so grateful.

I endured January and the following February 2019 I went back to the UK and picked up my son and the very pregnant mother of his baby. We drove back down to the Gers where they spent the last few weeks of her pregnancy.

They were tempted to stay. We even found a sage femme (midwife). I love that it's translated wise woman in French, but in the end my daughter in law, (she's technically not but I see her as if she is) felt that she would be more confident giving birth in a British hospital. I think if they could have stayed that would have decided the question for me to stay and make my life in France but when they left I felt alone again.

So I decided renting a flat in town may be the answer. The farm sold quickly, much to the surprise of all parties, so either way I would have to move. The new incumbents had lots of horses so mine staying on would not be possible and they also wanted the gites for their family.

I found a characterful if quirky apartment in an ancient building right in the centre of Eauze. Still obsessed with getting back on the Chemin, I also found there was a lovely livery yard right by the chapel on the point at Manciet where we started the ride and lost the horses on that first day.

I decided I would move my horses there once the French farm was sold and despite my hesitation to furnish an old French apartment, this was to be my future in France. One day on my drive home from town, as I circled the roundabout, I was distressed to see that one of the two scruffy dogs was lying prone and lifeless at the edge of the road. Devastated, but not surprised by the inevitability of its death, I sobbed all the way home consoling myself with the thought that Scruffy 1 had died doing what he loved most, chasing juggernauts. It didn't stop my sadness and grief at the loss though. I felt sadness for his mate Scruffy 2 also.

I got on with arrangements to move myself and my horses to what seemed a more sociable environment: the livery yard on the trail with fabulous hacking and the grandiose but somewhat dilapidated apartment above cafes and overlooking the square and cathedral of Eauze.

Even in those days before Brexit, the French estate agent seemed somewhat suspicious of foreigners and demanded the full payment of six months rent upfront. This made me hesitate as being of a nomadic character I do not care for commitment. I said I'd let him know and went home to think about it.

On the way home both Scruffy 1 and 2 chased my wheels and I realised that another of their party tricks was just playing dead. I was delirious with relief and joy.

I got through until March and was looking forward to spring and having a bit more life in town although I was already planning on living between France and the UK.

One morning in March 2019, whilst my friend Lara was visiting me, I went out to the paddock to find a completely lame Salvador.

He was literally unable to walk and it became obvious after a few days that this was serious. Not only this, a small squamous cell tumour on his penis had started to grow rapidly and was not responding to any treatment . His leg got a bit better but it was with deep sadness that it started to dawn on me that my riding days on him were curtailed, if not over. As charming as Eauze was, I could see no point in staying with a lame horse in a yard on the Chemin St Jacques I couldn't ride on and a flat full of furniture in a France that was rapidly running out for me.

With one retired old boy, Patriot, and one that I needed some support with, Warpaint and the fact that I had not managed to sell my house with land, I decided to go back to the UK. And thank goodness I did, as unbeknown to me not just one, but two grandchildren were on their way.

CHAPTER 6

BABIES, BREXIT AND COVID

The reality of settling in Eauze when I had grandchildren on the way just came a bit too late for me.

On top of this my safe riding horse Salvador was injured and had a growing skin tumour. The French vet had diagnosed his lameness as a ruptured tendon-a pretty catastrophic injury with no visible cause. There was no way I was going to be riding him again for a while.

On 30th March 2019, my grandson, Rain Bronz Levy-So made his appearance in The John Radcliffe hospital in Oxford just as I arrived home. I stayed 5 days to welcome the newborn and then after filling the fridge for them in my apartment where they were staying, headed back to France where I did my packing. All the horse stuff went into the Land Cruiser and trailer, which was to be picked up and driven back to England on 15th April by Andy, a retired English driver, living in France. I'd booked him on the night crossing from Le Havre to Portsmouth. The horses were going by professional transporter and all the rest went into the BMW ready for me to leave as soon as the horse lorry had been.

There followed a few nail-biting days, organising the paperwork for the French export licences and the veterinary approval for Hunter to return to the UK. I had to drive to Auch, the prefecture town of the department of the Gers, not once but twice, to submit the horses passports and licences and then again for the veterinary papers but eventually they were all cleared to leave the next morning at 9am.

That lunchtime I got a call from Andy who had left that morning. Did I have breakdown insurance? My heart sank. There was a terrible noise in the background. At that moment I could have cursed the person who told me that there was no need for breakdown on a Toyota Land Cruiser as "they never break down"!

The Land Cruiser had indeed broken down on the roadside at the edge of a place called St Maixent l'Ecole, halfway up France. Badly too, as when he called me I could barely hear him for the grinding noise it was making. I did think he must have been going like the clappers to get there so quickly. Andy thought it might be the differential lock? He managed to get it into Monnet Automobiles in the town where he abandoned it and since there was, luckily for him, a train station I got him a train ticket home for £70 and that was the end of him. However, my stuff inside the horsebox was also abandoned.

On the morning of 16th of April my horses were picked up by equine transporters ETA. Salvador was still very lame but luckily he had been pronounced fit to travel and they gave him his own mobile stable at the front of the lorry.

I now had to drive up via St Maixent both to pick up anything crucial, like horse medicines and feeds as well as talk to the garage about repairing it. I swung by St Maixent l'Ecole a few hours later and saw my Land Cruiser parked out the front, my trailer had been locked in a yard around the back for security. I went into the office and again proceeded to challenge my French autopart vocabulary to discuss the repairs with them. It was indeed the differential lock and I was horrified to learn it would be between 5000 -8000 euros to repair. The vehicle was probably only worth about £1500 as it was old and had 160,000 miles on the clock but it was the most useful workhorse and I was deeply attached to it despite it being a gas guzzler.

I was gutted and had no choice but to pack what I could into my car then abandon it and tell them just to hang onto it whilst I sped back to the UK to organise something. What an additional hassle!

The horses arrived back in Devon on 18th April 2019, none the worse for wear after their journey. In fact leading them off the monstrous lorry and up the narrow Devon lane back home they were extremely spirited, even Salvador had a spring in his lame step.

It was a relief to be back but I no longer had a home to move back into because, since I was not planning on returning, I had tenants in my house on the basis that they were going to buy the place as soon as their apartment in London was sold, which it was not doing as quickly as it should have. There was also a friend with her two children living in the annex.

So in order to be close to my horses and given it was early May, the very best time of year to be on Dartmoor, and soon be summer, rather than go back to my now husbandless apartment in Oxford, I decided to stay in my tack room, the rustic, wooden cabin on my yard with a log burning stove, a burbling brook behind it to lull me to sleep and to wake up to see my horses in the field scented with bluebells.

Life was relatively easy and calm after France. My son and his partner and baby had moved into a flat in Modbury, a small Devon town near the sea about a half hour's drive away. They had adopted an enormous, lollopy rescue dog from France that was obsessed with chasing a ball and we met for walks with the baby and dogs on the windswept moor. I had money coming in from lodgers and tenants. I lived with few mod cons in my cabin, showered at the leisure centre, went to the laundrette and saw friends and family. I felt a sense of relief at coming home despite missing the beauty of France.

Salavador was stable, no longer visibly lame at the walk although his leg was still big and puffy. I cut hedgerow herbs for him, comfrey, cleavers and meadowsweet. He was also having photonic red light therapy weekly and daily applications of frankincense and other oils on the tumour and he seemed to be happy enough, not that he was what I would call a very happy, extroverted soul like for example my mare Opal. Some horses are just obviously more visibly happy than others and it is the subject of another inquiry but I do think horses, like people, have issues of trauma that affect their mood and happiness and Salvador was obviously traumatised. Or maybe he was just shy and wary of humans and who could blame him? Having been to Argentina myself one can only imagine the way horses like him, a common or garden ranch horse, are treated?

In June I took a short trip to Spain to celebrate my nephew's birthday. The weather there in June on the Costa Blanca is always so lovely and we had a few nice days with my parents and Aunt and her new rather elderly husband. As I went to the airport to drop them off I got a call from the pet sitter. She was worried about Salvador saying she thought he was struggling to urinate.

Within half an hour the vet I called arrived to see him. I felt powerless to do anything but worry as I still had a few days away. It took me straight back to the time I had been in Spain in 2016 when Salvador colicked really badly, the miraculous recovery from which had pressed the go button on this trip.

Here I was again in Spain and the vet needed to come. Was it something about Spain I wondered?

Thank heavens I had at least done it. I had achieved my dream with my lovely Argentine Criollo in a short window of the couple of years where he was healthy. Now here we were again with the vet talking about surgery as being the only option, which luckily he had not needed back then, and would cost at least £6000 now to amputate the poor guy's penis which the vet said might sort it. I immediately decided I would not be putting him through that and I returned home to arrange for Salvador to be humanely put to sleep.

The next few days were filled with dread. It was upsetting because it was not just the pain of the loss of my beloved horse who had carried me around uncomplainingly for so many years, but also the loss of the potential to continue the dream with him that was my ongoing ride through France.

I could not face being there when he died and went for a walk by the sea but my neighbour Caroline bravely stood at his side for which I am grateful.

The only thing that kept me from falling into a hole of grief about him were the certainty that it was his time to leave and the memories that we had up till now made on our travels. Horses are not as attached to being alive as we are. It's not that animals don't fight to stay alive-of course they do-but sometimes they have had enough and are ready to let go and cross the rainbow bridge. I comforted myself with this, even if it isn't true, and I know I did my best for him over the years since he first emerged on this continent in Italy, bedraggled and scraggly from that, one can only imagine, terrible, six week boat journey from Argentina.

As it was he passed away before we had finished the mission of completing the trail as far as St Jean Pied de Port. The thing about riding a trail like the St Jacques is that once you're on the trail you just want to keep going anyway, so St Jean was an arbitrary but logical ending, however had we got there we would probably have wanted to continue to Santiago anyway.

So either way Vicki and I still had the unfinished business to get to St Jean Pied de Port but now I had lost my horse and my life was firmly rooted back in the UK. Over the next few months the idea slipped onto the back burner.

No one could have predicted all the things that happened to make it slip so far away. Not only the loss of my horse, but Vicki also incredulously lost her beloved Mouse to colic at the age of 25, meaning that she now only had the one riding horse, Q so I couldn't even go over and ride with her now was I able to

In August that year there was a huge summer storm . I was cosy in my cabin and didn't even hear it, but in the night a huge beech tree uprooted and fell on the house. It missed my lodger's head by a few minutes as her sofa was underneath the part of the roof it crashed through and she had gone late to bed.

I was shaken by the whole incident. My lodger had to move out but the tenants stayed. There followed extensive repairs mainly to the barns which were damaged. I felt I could no longer be responsible for lodgers and tenants and such a huge, wild property and I couldn't wait for them to sell their flat and buy it.

Luckily In September they got an offer on their place and made me an offer which I reluctantly accepted as it was short of my asking price but I was keen to sell now, still dreaming of a life abroad with my horses. Although the lethal wind had been a southerly and the trees were in full leaf, which was less stable, everytime the wind blew, which it does a lot up there in the Northwest direction of the property, I lay awake imagining another tree crashing down.

In October my purchasers pulled out of the sale just prior to exchange of contracts, due to a rethink of the amount of money they felt they would have to spend on the property. They found another cheaper house and moved out .I wish they would have had their reality check sooner. Over the years my lovely property has attracted a lot of dreamers who have had so many creative projects for the place but ultimately lacked the funds to restore and maintain it.

In the end I moved back into my home. It was kind of a relief. I felled or topped any of the neighbouring trees that could do serious damage. Those ancient beeches were coming to the end of their lives and were susceptible to fungus, which had caused the failure of the big tree that did so much damage. It looked healthy enough, you couldn't see the root damage underneath until the giant was laying prone across the garden and the roof of my house.
There followed a lot of repair and restoration work to the house and gardens.

In January 2020 I made a trip to Japan with my daughter Holly, to visit her brother Brave, my son, and other little grandson who had been born in Kobe. I'm glad we did as in March 2020 Covid arrived and closed all travel down just on my birthday, the day he arrived home from Japan with his baby and partner. I'm so glad they decided to leave Japan then in order to be more accessible to the family, as it would have been impossible to see them again for a long, long time. Movement was severely curtailed for months. I was therefore happy to be living back in my house again, despite having wanted to sell it for years. It proved a respite for us all.

In February my older son Silver, his partner, toddler and large, lollopy rescue dog moved into the house as they had to leave their flat in Modbury due it being damp and mouldy and generally unfit for a little boy's health, a common enough problem in UK rented housing that landlords like to ignore or even blame tenants for, but it kills children and I didnt want my grandson to become sick. Now I had both my sons and grandsons staying with me. So instead of the lonely isolation I might have endured in lockdown, far from the madding crowd, I had instead a warm, cosy and fun filled life with babies and dogs. How fortunate I was too to be able to ride Warpaint out on the empty moor behind the house.

I know a lot of people suffered terribly in lockdown especially in towns and cities but there on Dartmoor, tucked away with my sons and their families, my life was blissful as it's a quiet rural life anyway.

Luckily none of us caught Covid at this time and we didn't come into contact with many people, so much so that I was always shocked by my weekly outing to Tesco Extra to see people wearing masks and queuing. I spent my time being a grandma to toddlers, riding and writing comedy and did a Zoom comedy writing course every Tuesday evening which kept my brain going .

It was so fortuitous that I had fairly recently managed to get a reasonable internet connection up there after twenty years of remonstrating with BT, but to no avail. We were the forgotten rural dwellers, that had neither broadband width nor even a mobile signal. Even the landline calls sounded as if you were drowning. Imagine! After years of frustration not even being able to watch Youtube without glitches, my lovely next door neighbour found a deal that involved putting a very tall pole up in my field with an antenna facing a very specific angle that actually worked. In the early days it blew down a bit and twisted away from the signal but eventually he stabilised it and we could stream and zoom and watch Netflix at last.

It was actually life changing. That and the fact that I found a ford that crossed the river at an impenetrable part of the moor near me, that led me to the next common on the moor, and opened up long rides for me without having to go on the road. My house on Dartmoor was a constant love hate tug. I hated the winters and the isolation and burden of dealing with things going wrong alone but loved the springs and early summers when it might even be dry enough to do a long ride on the moor. My main and only reason for being there was the riding but I had got bored of the same rides. This is why I had gone to France in the first place as I love a variety of scenery and culture. To combine my love of horse riding and travel was and is heaven for me. But now in that summer of lockdown, I loved being there again and it was dry and sunny too for the most mostpart. But I still had a degree of restlessness. Eventually in July we were briefly let out of lockdown and me and my sister, who also had cabin fever, made a quick trip to Spain. We paddled in the Mediterranean and ate nice tapas, albeit only on a terrace, but since Spain is well equipped for outdoor eating it was no issue. This time, to my great relief, no horse emergency related call or ailment interrupted my holiday.

In my opinion, Brexit was an act of total national self-harm. How we could have let an advisory referendum firstly even happen at all and secondly be the basis for ruining our economy and many people's individual lives, I can never fully understand?

I can only attribute it to manipulation of the fears of British people, that were stoked and fuelled by right wing elements in our society and ended up with no benefit whatsoever to anyone except disaster capitalists, ultra right wingers and the rich who profit from duping ordinary folks. How easy and untrue to circulate the idea that it was the EU who was the enemy destroying national sovereignty. I still feel choked up about it not the least because taking animals to the EU is now a major endeavour and prohibitively costly.

On Christmas you always think about next year's holiday and this one was no exception. Riding in France now became a distinct possibility again, not on my own horse Warpaint this time due to Brexit but Vicki had purchased another Connemara called Baltic. She offered me to ride her other horse Q and we avidly discussed riding trails together.

It still hung over us that we had not completed our original mission of getting to St Jean Pied de Port. We looked at lots of possible trail routes but decided nothing

would really make sense till we had achieved the route to St Jean and could put the Pilgrims trail behind us,
We decided to set off in Spring at the very end of April and spent weeks researching stops and Gites that would take horses. Getting the route, dates and places on the trail co-ordinated was a major task but eventually we had every night booked both for the horses and ourselves. A lot of flights were being cancelled at this time so I had my fingers crossed.

But at the beginning of 2022 my father, who was approaching his 96th birthday, suddenly started to go downhill. His mobility was bad and he now struggled to walk more than a few steps and very slowly at that. He was getting very frail and his Parkinson's disease, which had not really affected his brain until now, made activities with him much harder.

Travelling, which he had always loved, was becoming too difficult for them as he would get confused and lose things and make mistakes. He would still talk about going to Spain or whatever but you could see it couldn't happen. Even when my Mum took him only as far as Bournemouth at Easter 2022 they had a terrible time coping.

That was the end of his travels and the end of my trip to France. I just didn't feel I could leave her alone with him at this time so I decided not to go and we spent ages rebooking the whole trip for the first week of June, which was really the last window before it got too hot in France and the flies start to be intolerable to the horses. I sent emails to all the gite hosts apologising that we had to postpone and managed to rebook dates. All without exception were sympathetic to me and told me to be with my Dad.

Mum was beside herself with the responsibility of looking after him. At the age of 90 she couldn't be expected to be a full time carer for her ailing husband. There is no way to dress up the sufferings of old age and of course it is a privilege denied to many to grow old, but it's upsetting for those close to the one who is preparing to leave.

The June ride never happened either because Dad swelled up with fluid on his kidneys and had to be admitted to hospital for treatment. His delirium in there particularly at nights became great he kept talking about being in prison and he would shout out in the night, "Im Jewish" and apparently wandered around the ward and tried to discharge himself. He was not able to manage to use his phone unaided any more, but if he could get help he would call mum in the middle of the night and say "We've got no money left" or "The credit cards have gone".

Dad had been a 19 year old Jewish corporal in the British army in 1944 when he was sent to liberate Bergen-Belsen, the notorious Jewish concentration camp, where he experienced processing people who were living corpses. It was so bad that they had to burn the prisoner huts. The people were starving and riddled with disease.

This experience coloured his life but it was only in his latter years that he was able to articulate his experience, which he did with great clarity and wisdom, when interviewed by Natasha Kaplinsky for ITV for a Holocaust memorial tribute. Dad even went back to Bergen-Belsen and met the Queen on account of his heroism which he was too humble to claim.

Dad was a liberal minded and compassionate man who cared for his family deeply.

Fortunately after a week they discharged him. The hospital staff must have been relieved to see the back of him although they said not. But not before a handrail had been installed as Dad still had his bedroom upstairs, and a care package agreed, with carers coming in twice a day as mum was rightly anxious about being alone with him or dealing with the copious amounts of medication they had him on. It was a cause of stress and confusion for him.

I always wonder why they feel the need to dose old people up to the nines with drugs? I would have taken him off the lot but I was not empowered to make that decision. What is the worst that could happen to an obviously dying man?

I was adamant that Dad should not go into a home, despite the advancing care needs. I stayed over as often as I could at my parents house in a next door bedroom. However one night I woke up in the middle of the night to a huge crash. Dad lay prostrate on the floor. He was only a small man but I could barely pick him up. He fell three more times that night. At that point I knew we'd reached the end of the line with caring for him at home.

Luckily there is a fabulous nursing home at a retirement complex in my parents village and he was able to be admitted the next day. The place was lovely with good food and he had a nice room but it was of little interest to Dad as he didn't open his eyes again.

It was very sad but somehow when someone makes it to a peaceful enough death at the age of 96 in a life well lived, it is a cycle completed.

I was now free to go to France although to be honest I was almost over the whole idea and would not have bothered were it not for the encouragement of Vicki and that I had talked myself up into it and didn't want to let her down yet again.

CHAPTER 7

THE CHEMIN AGAIN

It was the last day of August 2022 after a parched and baking summer, leaving parks brown and fields looking like the Atacama desert. I see this below me from the aeroplane window of the last flight of the year out to Bergerac from Bristol and I breathe a sigh of relief that I am finally, finally en route to complete the mission we had to abandon four years ago , never for a moment contemplating that it would be another four years before we got back on the trail that was calling our names.

Vikki met me at Bergerac across the street from arrivals in their unmissable red and yellow, classic Deux Chevaux.

After a few stalls and splutters, the engine cranked up with gusto and off we drove, with of course a trip to Decathlon to stop by the Equestrian section, before arriving at Vicki's to meet the real 2 Chevaux, Q grandly known as Qulbuto de Lap and Baltic who also has a fancy name which I can't quite recall?

Vikki and Baz own a charming country cottage with horses and cats and a few acres of land in the pretty countryside of Lot and Garonne.

It was a three and a half hour drive down to the start of our trail and after a lot of fannying around, with Vikki packing the kitchen sink and me poo picking at the same time as trying to remonstrate with O2, who had annoyingly cut off my automatic EU roaming and wouldn't even answer the call, at around 11am we clambered aboard the loaded vehicle and set off. Given the amount of stuff and animals we had loaded on there it was a miracle the truck moved at such speed.

Mid afternoon, after a stop at a Boulangerie where the simple portion of chips I fancied, grandiosely marketed as hot food, were finished or had more likely never been on, we arrived at our first stop of Argagnon, a restful abode, a pilgrims Gite with shepherds huts (roulottes) in the amazing gardens and grounds in an otherwise charmless village dissected, as are so many in France, by a remorseless main road.

Day 1 to Argagnon.

Finding horse accommodation situated exactly on the Chemin St Jacques is a bit of a challenge but this place was a lucky find as apart from the danger of being knocked down in the 30 seconds you are on this road, there's a well worn walking path goes alongside, and although you can hear the road and the motorway, the A60 which is somewhere very close by, there was plenty of room for horses. The horses were very irritated by flies and I was the welcome new blood for the hordes of vicious mosquitos lurking in the woods around the roulottes.

We planned to stay here for 3 nights. The first being our arrival night, then on the second day we needed to leave the horses at the Gite and head down to the end of our ride at St Jean Pied de Port, right in the foothills of the Pyrenees, close by what is the Spanish border, divided by language, although it is actually the former kingdom of Navarre and before that the kingdom of Pamplona, deep in the Basque country which links France and Spain   historically and culturally. We had arranged with the final Gite of the trail there to park the truck and trailer for the end of our ride.

Our very charming host Nicholas, back at Argagnon, had erected a rather slack fence for us in between welcoming exhausted and thirsty pilgrims whose first urgent mission was to wash their socks and get them on the line whilst the sun was still fierce.

Dinner that night was a communal meal at a long table outside, with several other guests, mostly middle aged, all French and all walking the Chemin. They came from as far north as Normandy and west from Lyon. I tried to chat and join in, getting the gist but not the detail.

What we ate was some coarse pate, I guessed out of a tin, followed by a mound of tinned haricot beans with carrots and some chunks of some kind of unrecognisable meat, possibly pork. It was better food than served on Celebrity in the Jungle, but only just.

At the end was cake and thin slices of cheese which redeemed the meal a bit or would have if I ate either? A very kind guest shared her gluten- free crackers and sheeps cheese with me, telling me in no uncertain terms that I would have to notify the Gites of my food quirks weeks, if not months, even years, ahead so they could accommodate my diet. I guess there's no popping out to Tesco or Sainsbury local to pick up Free- from supplies? After the meal the host Nicholas played banjo for us, including Irish songs and gave a talk on the history and origins of the banjo in French. It was interesting and everyone loved the music, or at least they seemed to. One of the pilgrims was the spitting image of Miriam Margolyes, which was funny as the aforesaid had recently been filmed walking it and here she was again or so made a joke about .

It was lovely sitting outside in the evening, sipping wine but I was being ravaged by hordes of vicious mosquitos lurking in the woods around the roulottes.

It rained hard in the night, yet in the morning after a long, hot, dry summer, the ground was barely even damp.

We therefore decided to use Day 2 to transport the trailer as it was overcast and muggy and thunderstorms were forecast. In the end they weren't terrible but still we would have got a soaking. We had hummed and hawed, well about everything really, but certainly about which day to do the loop and which day to take the trailer down? In the end I think we got it right as we missed the rain and once we did set out we could go full steam ahead although as it turned out full steam was quite slow once the packs were loaded on.

The drive down to St Jean was over an hour and very pretty. I couldn't wait to ride it.

Getting back to Argagnon and the horses from the gite at Lasse was itself a mission which involved hiking back down to St Jean, getting on one of the only two daily buses to St Palais, waiting 3 hours in St Palais, a fairly sizeable town, for our connecting bus to Orthez and then blagging a lift back with Nicholas who sent updates throughout the day as to the state of the horses.
"Your barbies are fine" he endearingly said and "Waiting for you to come".

But they were not settled on that first day and with the heat and the flies they were definitely questioning why the hell they had been abandoned in a small, hot paddock and Baltic, who used to be a show jumper, could easily scale the loose ,makeshift fence to get into the huge field they were adjacent to, had he wanted, so Nicolas found a battery for the fence as ours was in the trailer en route to St Jean for the field at the end of the ride, as we discovered over the next days, were so many of the things we needed. Even though they were restless and obviously couldn't see the purpose of why they were left in a strange field they respected the fence so had to stay put, hence the sweet text from our host putting our minds at rest.

We arrived on bus 1, a small bus with no one on it, except us, at St Palais at 1.30 pm, the plan being to have lunch during the excessive interlude of a 3 hour wait in St Palais, which's limited charms did not extend to that long, and to gather supplies for the ride and lunch.

But this was after all France and although in no other country I can think of in the world would you be turned away from a restaurant at 1.30, except possibly Spain where it's still too early, the response everywhere was 'Trop tard', too late.

Too late for lunch and it was only 1.30pm! Surely we could not be punished for the fact that the French only have a bit of bread and jam for their breakfast? But they are merciless when it comes to the hours of dining, especially lunch. Even the bakeries close. Finally we found a brasserie and by agreeing to have the only dish there was left and instantly sitting down, we managed to blag a fairly decent lunch. However to my horror it was veal which I won't eat under compassionate grounds, it having not enjoyed much life at all. The chef actually made me a steak frites which together with a glass of dry white Basque wine eased the 3 hour wait and even made it quite tolerable. This is the thing I find with the French, after being abrupt and dismissive in the

101

first instant, if you kowtow, they end up being quite pleasant.

The afternoon bus, bus 2, was a big one, yet again with no passengers except us and the only other passenger on Bus 1,a rather unkempt old man who had remained at the bus stop chuntering for the whole 3 hour wait. We went through several pretty little Bearn towns with no one getting on or off at any of numerous stops until almost the last before Orthez where our host Nicolas kindly picked us up from the station.

We returned to the Gite to find the horses still in the field being annoyed by flies and looking no more impressed with their surroundings.

That night there was only one other guest. A German pilgrim, Jurgen, who had walked all the way from his home on the Polish border. He had been walking for four months and staying at churches which he said are apparently obligated to provide sanctuary for pilgrims. He was hard core compared to us who had not yet even started our trail. We felt like frauds.

Dinner was once again the same tinned pate and hey ho, tinned haricots verts with the bit of unnameable meat. Maybe it was last nights reheated or maybe it was a new one? Either way my substantial lunch allowed me to politely decline dinner that night and I had some rice cakes and by now extremely smelly goats cheese and ate and then in turn, gave myself over to the mosquitoes for their nightly feast.

We had now been here two days and I had not yet got on the horse I was going to ride. I started to get silly anxieties that I may fall off and end up in a French hospital.

Day 2 *The loop to Arthez de Bearn*

It's interesting how attachment to an idea can ruin the present moment.

As soon as I got on my horse Q the following morning for the first time I had ever ridden him, as we swung on out of the Gite I wanted to never end the ride.
Sitting back on a horse on the long trail, I felt at home in my soul again.

I was already thinking how can I keep doing this for the rest of my life? Can I ride through Spain and Portugal next? Will she sell me this horse(very unlikely)? Could I buy a horse and keep him in Europe? Could I take people on horseback on the Camino? What about bringing my horse over after bloody Brexit?

But in plotting and planning ways to extend this feeling of unparalleled freedom and joy bursting through me, I was flirting with the danger of missing the wonder of the present moment. As fear started to arise that I may be getting too old for such adventures, time is running out as my body is not as strong or supple, bones become brittle, injuries hurt more and may not heal and my body is not the comfortable, padded cushion it was, blah blah blah, I started to feel sad at the thought of my desires receding into the pit of unfulfilled dreams . Yet just as here I was fulfilling them!

So I just breathed and rested deeply in my saddle for a few kilometers and all was soon well again with the universe. That's my kind of meditation.

Yesterday had been a non-riding day as we'd had to take the trailer down to the end of the ride laden with fencing posts as requested by our host there although looking at the lush mountain grass down there I doubted they'd stray.

So today was the official start of our ride looping up to Arthez de Bearn where we left off in 2018 and coming back down on the Camino. We rode down to the same meadow we had camped at with two different horses and of course they had no idea that here their predecessors had spent the night and we had pitched our tent and eaten baked beans as the only restaurant was boarded up and still is. The figs were as ripe on the tree today as they had been back then and both me and Q snacked on them although we didn't tell Vicki.

Then off through the sleepy town for old times sake, grabbing a ride-through coffee from the same grumpy barman and riding back to our Gite for the 3rd night where we encountered some interesting people walking on the Camino.

Today was a short,easy ride as we didn't have to carry saddle bags and were back home for lunchtime which is just as well as it was nice to consolidate what went in which pannier, as well as rest a bit and I was covered in mosquito bites, to which there seemed to be no solution in pharmacy, neither natural nor chemical, other than to let them have free rein with me.

We had hoped to find dinner in the village of Argagnon and thereby avoid the green bean repeat. By this time we realised that there was only one menu and pilgrims are not as fussy as us. We walked along the hot, busy main road but there was no restaurant, only a bar -tabac.

These are essentially tobacconists with tables and a coffee machine that serve drinks and if you're lucky something to eat? We were not. I asked for cold water but there was no water, apparently there were shortages of bottled water in France according to the proprietress. Neither was there ice cream despite the board with pictures of it. I settled for a peach juice which was at least served chilled and Vikki had a beer.

At the thought of eating the dinner at the Gite or starving we quickly messaged the owner and cheekily asked for a vegetarian alternative. It's not as if he was slaving in the kitchen. Nicolas had so many charms and talents as a host but cooking was not one of them. But to our surprise and delight that night we were served scrambled eggs and the most delicious tomatoes I have ever eaten whilst the other pilgrims duly ate their pate and green beans, without the faintest idea that the menu never changes.

Occasionally pilgrims brought their own food and there was a young couple from La Reunion who had their own appetising looking food that they said they had purchased at the village shop at Masclat which we would pass when we set off the next morning on the ride proper. That evening the banjo was brought out and the same songs were played but the difference is that tonight's guests danced and got quite vocal.

Day 3 Sauvelade.

The first proper day of the Chemin started out with a main road, a motorway crossing and a train track too. The flies were on the early shift and Vicki's saddle bags were slipping to the left.

At the shop at Masclat we stopped but the horses were agitated by flies and wouldn't be tied up or stand still so I had to go in and out quickly. I'd have loved a coffee sitting at the shady tables outside but it was a question of speed, never easy in a French village store, where things have to be weighed and someone in front of you is chatting to the shop lady.

I managed to grab an avocado, some peaches, some ham, mayonnaise in a far too big container for my pack and cotton wool pads, as I thought, quite rightly as it turned out, we might get some rubbing and chafes and some chewing gum which was an impulse buy that annoyed me by getting stuck to the packet and making a fair old mess in my saddle bag.

It was a long morning's trek past more industrial sized maize farms and dead sunflowers. There was also quite a lot of roadwork. You'd imagine the Compostelle to be a grassy path leading all the way from Le Puy en Velay to Santiago de Compostela but in reality it's a lot of paths joined up by a lot of D roads. Fortunately they are mostly quiet and traffic free but there are sections of very busy main roads and even crossings, some rather dangerously placed on the brow of a hill on fast moving roads. With a heavy pack on your back you may have to run for your life if one of those juggernauts suddenly appears at speed. This is why I wore my gilet jaune (yellow vest) at all times.

But this morning was mostly off road and at one point we were passed by the daily appearance of a grumpy old farmer in an old car bumping up the track, who stopped to shout out of his window something like ,"Ce n'est pas le Compostelle pour chevaux" which was either a question is this suitable for horses, or more likely a judgement on us riding horses on the path through these fields.

Either way we ignored him and rode on and he bumped off up the track.

Although it was only 12 kilometers to our stop for the night it seemed longer and we only got to have a very quick standing lunch as the horses would not stand still.

At the Abbaye of Sauvelade we took a wrong turn as the Gite signpost was overgrown and faded and ended up riding 2 kms further, picking up a loose hunting dog who relentlessly followed us, which was a worrying responsibility as it was all along the main road. Someone finally appeared and pointed us the way where we had already been to no avail but Madame at the Gite, an eccentric, deeply Béarnaise version of Gina Lollobridgida, appeared in an old van to guide us but promptly drove off before we found the route, the sign of which was yet again obscured. Eventually we found the house and were ordered to tie our horses up and be Zen but that doesn't work with our horses who wouldn't stand still because of flies. Neither did we conveniently have a fence with us, so after much altercation, they got put in with some rather bemused Blonde Aquitaine cows and calves in the field, apparently belonging to a cousin.

We were not permitted to bring our saddle packs into the house as they had "Been in the woods". I don't know what kind of diseases she thought we might be carrying on them but she was adamant. Given that she herself had a terrible cold and cough, which we were convinced was due to her heavy smoking but she insisted it was because she had inhaled chemicals from cleaning the swimming pool, it therefore seemed a bit rich to force us to leave all our "infected" possessions in the garage. We were given cloth bags to put our essentials in.

"You take only what you need, no more!" ordered Nadette. We were tired and thirsty and the obligatory mint or citron syrup with water served on arrival had to be drunk before being let into the maison.

The old Bearnaise house was nevertheless delightful. My bedroom was obviously the master suite with a huge old oak door. It was quirky, with creaky ancient wood floors. The bath and toilet were in the bedroom with no door nor even screen to separate it, so luckily I had my own room and the window had a tall palm tree outside in that colonial fashion. It had a balcony on the top floor with a decorative balustrade overlooking the horse and cow field, a swimming pool and gardens full of fruit and vegetables including wild peach trees, aubergines, peppers, tomatoes and chilis.

Our hostess Nadette spent the afternoon cooking, coughing and making a terrible mess in the kitchen whilst Vicki had a swim in the freezing pool and I caught up on my social media posts.

Eventually showered and refreshed, apero was served at 7 followed by dinner which was actually a nice, home cooked meal of souffle followed by a vegetable bake albeit a bit cheesy for me and a homemade cake for Vicki with Chantilly- whipped cream- and for me a wild peach fruit salad oozing with peach juice and sweet liquor.

I slept the sleep of the dead despite the itchy bites and the next morning after a lot of faffing with repacking our saddle bags whilst trying not to re-enter the house because we didn't want to keep taking our boots off, we set off for Navarrenx. But not before Nadette had pulled us both into a warm, smoky embrace thereby enhancing our chances of catching her germs.

Day 4 Navarrenx

The next day dawned cool and a bit grey which was just as well as we had a winding 14.5 kilometer ride to Navarrenx, an 11th century fortified town with a castle and a church that has housed both Catholics and at one time Protestant worshippers.

Of course we got to see none of them as the horses were as usual fully demanding of all our attention but we stopped for a lunch break at the grassy remparts at the entrance to town and also a supermarket,a well stocked Carrefour Express, where I loaded up on supplies I couldn't then fit into my saddle packs, whilst Vicki held the horses outside and rather sweetly, the Gendarmes came to say hi and stroke them. Not only did we manage to shop but we even rode past a cashpoint where I dismounted and got some euros. .

The sun came out strongly as we arrived at Castetnau Camblong. Domaine de la Castagnere was a most beautiful house with a convivial host with chickens and ducks and horses and sheep running everywhere. Again there was a bit of altercation and a chaotic moment whilst the resident horses decided to escape and give the visiting horses the once over but all soon settled down. Here we got a well earned massage and la Bonne Cuisine. I was only persuaded to lift my lifelong aversion to eating foie gras when the host informed me that far from being the force fed bird I feared, with a tube strapped to its gullet, it was the forebear of one of these squawking and very free range birds. It was absolutely delicious and of course I won't eat commercially produced foie gras but I have to say it was phenomenal.

The rooms were charming and creative, although I felt a bit sorry for the other guest, a jovial German gynaecologist walking the Chemin who had booked the oddball Bedouin room, which was essentially a yurt inside the house, very quirky and pretty but at the same time with only canvas walls he would be woken by us passing in the night on our endless trips to the bathroom, especially given that we drank a lot of wine.

We could never leave early enough. There was too much faffing with saddle packs and getting everything just right. It was such a learning curve about long distance trail riding in the heat, choosing the right tack, the right attachments, there's no such thing as too many carabiners.

We had left the numnahs out to dry in the sun but forgot to put them away at night. It had been so dry every night but this morning a heavy, early Autumn dew had soaked them in the early hours. Q also had a bit of a sore on his haunch from where the saddle bag, which was not protected by his everyday numnah, rubbed. We needed a longer Western type one. I had to ask the host if he had an old blanket or something longer to put under Q's hind bags? He brought me a very old bed sheet which Q fetchingly modelled for the rest of the trip, together with Nadette's old belt; the two of them cut a dashing equine image.

After our slow start, we had a lovely Sunday morning forest ride through the cool, leafy glades of the forest outside of Castetnau Camblong, stopping for water that the horses did not trust, spouting from an ancient tap into a stone trough.

We made good time nevertheless, despite the slow start and looked like we would still meet the self-imposed deadline of our latest desired time of arrival of 1500 hrs, looking forward to divesting ourselves of horses and tack, kicking back and a swim. And indeed we arrived after a long, hot ride via a hilltop high above the most idyllic valley at the Gite Bellevue at Aroue bang on time at 1500 hours.

But it was the wrong Gite Bellevue and not only that, the one we had booked was over 4 hours away, nowhere near the Compostelle we were following. The Gite Bellevue we arrived at were extremely surprised by me saying we are here and denied having heard of our coming nor had space for us, as they had a party of Americans and certainly had no space for horses, or so they said. Meanwhile the other Gite Bellevue over 4 hours ride away was cooking our dinner. It was a moment of great anxiety as our horses, especially Q who was opinionated, thought enough was enough. We felt awful about the mistake. The old folks at the wrong Gite Bellevue pointed us down the hill gesticulating towards a farm. We never found the farm but there was a communal Gite, very neat, very tidy, the ladies there were extremely head shaking about the horses saying they didn't have anywhere. I asked if they could go with the cows but was told 'non non non' as the horses could spread disease to the cows and vice versa, a thought that had not occurred to Nadette and her cousins' lovely cows.

Luckily my French is good and I managed eventually to evoke sympathy for our plight so a cousin was again found- there's always a relative with land- with a tiny field below where the horses could go. It was impossible to find or open the gate so at least I was reassured that they couldn't escape however there was no water, so we had to carry 6 buckets of water and some of the cows hay.

Vicki and I got a dormitory but to my relief there were only the two of us in there. We rented clean sheets and I even made the deadline to get my pyjamas washed by the ladies at the gite.

The relief was palpable but my adrenaline levels had been elevated and although we had a great night and supper with about 30 other pilgrims walking the Chemin at the communal table, who seemed rather bemused if not a little impressed, by two white horses being ridden on their same trail, I could neither fall asleep nor relax because I was so itchy and playing over and over the events of the afternoon. Communal gites generally have a silence code after 2130 as pilgrims go to bed early and get up whilst it's still dark so we had to be quiet but it was hard to silence our minds as we were wired out.

I can safely say it's faster on foot than on a horse. Horses are a lot of responsibility; finding them food and water, giving enough grazing breaks and managing sores, not to mention finding suitable enclosures for them at night? The day was only a short distance of 18 kilometers but it felt like 100 in 32°. The mosquitos were still relentlessly attacking me, they moved off my legs to my arms and fingers and I was bitten to shreds. The day was forecast to be 34° by afternoon and it was 24 kms. We had to leave early and all these pressures meant my eyes did not close from 11pm-6 am when I got up and on the road again.

Day 5 Ostabat- Asme

Attempting to leave early after a sleepless night at the communal gite in Aroue due to terrible itching mosquito bites and not being able to wind down after the palaver of being 4 hours away from the wrong Gite Bellevue and the brain- taxing task of begging for mercy in French, plus worry about the horses in a field on a dangerous bend, despite the impenetrable barbed wire, we got away just after 8am. Nothing could go wrong today could it?

A long morning's ride seemed to eat the kilometers now out of the beautiful Bearn and into the even more beautiful Basque. We were making good time and even caught up with some of the pilgrims from our gite who had left before us and we were looking forward to an afternoon with some catch up on rest, laundry and journal writing and even a swim in the Gîte's pool at Ostabat. We decided on a lunch stop at a picnic bench with a water fountain, however when we got there the pilgrims had nabbed the shady bench, leaving us only the one in plein soleil! We tied Baltic and Q to some smallish trees and sat down to eat some rather warm salads. You just cannot really get properly hydrated on a trip like this no matter how much you drink, and warm water just doesn't cut it. Before long, poor, silly Q pulled back and got in a paddy when the string didn't break and snapped his rope, banging his face and head. That was the end of our brief peace.

Only another 9 kms to go as we had already done 15kms before lunch. Leaving the village of Larribar-Sorhapuru we crossed a bridge over the river and there was a very steep trail up over some jagged stone steps. We negotiated these only to find a huge fallen tree laying across the track which the pilgrims on foot clambered over. There was no possibility for us to circumnavigate this obstacle due to deep drops on either side. There was nothing for it but to turn around and go all the way back to the village we had lunched at and find the road. Flagging down an old boy in a tractor, he showed us how to cut back down to the road via an old lady's garden which did not impress her and she came out, and once again my French had to be employed to explain our predicament. I don't think she understood a word of me at all, nor I of her, but we went through anyway and then had to ride to the next village Uhart-Mixe, along a scary main road with fast traffic going to St Palais and St Jean. Water for the horses was schlepped by Vicki from the cemetery. There was a sign for a bar but the bar was neither open nor even there. The only business was a taxi office which must do incredibly well in these remote parts. We sat in the shade of the bus shelter as we knew there were only two buses a day, having taken one ourselves a few days back. No one pooped thank heavens and we crossed a pedestrian crossing, which in France have no purpose as drivers don't stop, and then we saw a sign pointing back up to the chapelle we were supposed to have passed hours back.

After a steep, steep ascent, one of several, we finally made it onto something claiming to be the GR65 but was actually a newly tarmacked, melting road without a car on it. We literally went on forever on this track with high, dried mud banks until eventually we merged with the Chemin we should have been on. Trying not to be attached to either a rest or a swim we trudged on with the mission, only alleviated by the incredible scenery.

Late, late in the afternoon in about 34° we descended on the small hamlet of Harambeltz, which has a famous chapel, but the best thing for us was a donation cafe opposite with organic apple juice and biscuits and free fruit. The horses had apples and we had tea and juice and a cookie. Last bits of strength were mustered to ride on into Ostabat, a charming, mediaeval village in deeply Basque Country. I was almost crying riding through the village seeing people sitting outside drinking cold beers but we couldn't stop as neither would the horses ever stand still and allow us to do so, but more importantly time was against us. It was 530pm and we'd planned to be there for 2. We managed a quick swim after chucking the horses in a small secure field with lovely lush grass then straight to dinner where we met the party of Americans again, who shared their cold rose and turned out to be rather fun, with their tales of being double booked and the like. We were lucky as we had private rooms and even two showers, whereas they didn't and they were complaining. I slept all night with the fan on, which seemed to keep the new mosquitoes at bay although the itching from the past night's bites was still dreadful.

The next morning the Basque husband (I presumed) of the Gite owner sang us all Basque songs at breakfast about the pilgrims on the Chemin. I nearly cried. It was so moving but also quite funny. He insisted on being photographed with the horses.

Leaving the lovely Ferme "GAINEKO ETXEA" we were comforted by the fact we only had 24 kms to go to our final destination on the other side of St Jean Pied de Port, where our trailer was waiting. The self-imposed pressure was off.

But we were tired by now and the horses seemed tired and we had not really stopped to relax at all.

After a little bit of fannying around 3 kms along at Larceveau, listed as being the only place en route to get food, we deviated into the village only to find a) the shop was closed and b) we could have got there in minutes on the back chemin. I should have followed my gut!
I managed to blag a takeaway coffee au lait from the hotel which I filled my flask with. I don't normally have dairy but I thought the coffee might be too strong black. French coffee is a bit hit and miss as it can be too bitter for my liking. I also got a charcuterie sandwich, minus the bread, wrapped in foil, which lasted me for days. Off we set on the route which mostly followed high above the main road to St Jean. Again it seemed do-able by early afternoon despite the palaver of waiting for the bar to sort the coffee and food. But yet again, after going through two narrow, metal gates, the first we had come across on the trail and quite a way along a high ridge, there it was. Another fallen tree! This time there was no hesitation. We turned back all the way to a fountain we had stopped at about forty minutes before where the horses refused to drink.

It's annoying to have to keep dismounting at the water stops and untie the portable buckets to get water for them when even in the great heat they don't drink. Then suddenly after about 15 kms they are thirsty and will drink. It was also annoying to have to keep turning back on ourselves.

So from there we had to get on the main road which luckily had a slight protective strip we rode in and then there was a gate into the steepest field that we ascended and got back on the trail higher up. It was not quite as bad a diversion as the previous day but still long enough to add an hour and a half more on.

The afternoon was an endless trek up to Lacarre in about 32° and down to St Jean Le Vieux. It said it was only 8.1 kms to St Jean but I swear it was much longer. We just couldn't seem to get there. At the last few kilometers we lost the trail markers whilst talking about hot chocolate that we never had time to get. Besides, St Jean, which we just had to follow our noses to find, was the most heaving place imaginable with juggernauts and fast work traffic. We rode through in the rush hour heat with pilgrims on bridges taking photos and spooking the horses but we just gritted our teeth and rode on through the city walls. We were the true pilgrims and many pics of us were taken that afternoon. We felt like heroes but the horses were the actual heroes.

It was so dangerous there in the city traffic. One wrong move and it would have all been for nothing. But we made it. As we left St Jean to climb to the village where we were going with the horses, there on the bend I saw a bunch of people waving at us from a hotel pool. It was the Americans. They treated us as the celebrities we were but that's where it ended. As this was France we had to endure the indignity of being seen as tourists, queuing at the only restaurant open in a town of hundreds of visitors and automatically given an English menu. It was intense, emotional and incredible but I was by now fantasising about sleeping in my own bed and getting back to my own boring life.

A day off was needed and welcomed in St Jean during which we enjoyed the luxury of a vehicle to drive and hot chocolate, croissants and two dinners at the same restaurant with a waiter with a very strong Basque face, who could have been the twin brother of John de Florette, or even Cyrano de Bergerac, (Gerard Depardieu) and a fixed system of serving that involved not listening at all to the customer.

Although our gite was amongst the worst for comfort with a mattress that pinged when you sat on it, no sheets and more creatures inside the room than outside, it was silent and the air was fresh. Somehow I slept well the next two nights and we came to the end of our remarkable adventure.

I was very sad to say goodbye the next day to the two magical beauties Q and Baltic and their owner Vicki Drury. These two "fantastic beasts" carried us relentlessly, up and down the steep hills and wooded valleys that make up the Béarnaise and French Basque sections of the Chemin de Compostelle, thé St Jacques, which goes all the way from Le Puy en Velay in central France to Santiago de Compostela (or St Jacques) in Galicia Northern Spain. It crosses regions and borders all the while meandering from church to church and village to village. We have now ridden around 200 miles of this path and in total I have ridden around 300 miles since 2018 covering large tracts of France, which I only began to realise how much when we drove back up. I covered the area from the Limousin just below Limoges with Ruth Cox on her Gypsy Cob Ted and then several kilometers into and around the Lot and the Dordogne both alone and with Margie Brumby, then going down to the Gers where I stayed put over several hot and cooler months and rode miles around my village thereby discovering that the French Pilgrims trail passed a mere 10 kilometers from my accommodation.

This hatched the next plan and in September 2018 we set off from Manciet on the trail on an awe inspiring trek down the Chemin de Compostelle with a mission to reach St Jean pied de Port. However we failed to realise how far it was or how you have to limit your daily distances due to terrain, stopping to make sure the horses get enough grass for energy, relieving the weight of the tack and packs, the relentless flies and mosquitoes, obstacles and unforeseen circumstances of which we encountered several in the second leg of our epic journey. But we did it and I enjoyed a night of relative civilisation in Bordeaux, where a budget hotel seemed like a palace before flying to London in the morning.

A few months on and it's all slipping away from me; the sound of the bells in the high, green meadows around the necks of cows, donkeys and horses; the camaraderie on the trail at the communal Gites and shady stopping places along the trail from people all over the world, who are following the route with you and seem like old friends when you meet them again . I must confess I am feeling wistful about it all right now and deeply grateful for the experience. Of course going home and seeing my family and adorable grandchildren and my horses and Hunter is of great comfort especially over the winter which is the time to write, rest and restore energy ready for the Spring and the next adventure.

I don't know what's next? Who knows what's in store in these turbulent times? But even if I slip into a quiet retirement after this I can proudly call myself an Equestrian Traveller and maybe I'll just take up sewing or painting or rambling? Or maybe I'll just walk as much as possible and aim to ride on Dartmoor again next spring? Or maybe the

Napoleon trail or the Stevenson trail is beckoning? Just wanted to leave you with my story of an intense, blissful and quite challenging, at times, adventure and hope you've enjoyed it .

Setting out on Salvador

Hunter

The other Ruth

Arzacq-Arraziguet

The 3 boys at Caillaubert and the house.

Scruffy 1 and 2

Salvador artfully snacking on corn on the cob.

Our singing Basque host

Arriving in St Jean

Printed in Great Britain
by Amazon